> Nature's first green is gold,
> Her hardest hue to hold.
> Her early leaf's a flower;
> But only so an hour.
> Then leaf subsides to leaf.
> So Eden sank to grief,
> So dawn goes down to day.
> Nothing gold can stay.
>
> —Robert Frost, 1923

SECRETS from GRANDMA'S ATTIC

History Lost and Found
The Art of Deception
Testament to a Patriot
Buttoned Up
Pearl of Great Price
Hidden Riches
Movers and Shakers
The Eye of the Cat
Refined by Fire
The Prince and the Popper
Something Shady
Duel Threat
A Royal Tea
The Heart of a Hero
Fractured Beauty
A Shadowy Past
In Its Time
Nothing Gold Can Stay

SECRETS From GRANDMA'S ATTIC

Nothing Gold Can Stay

Becky Melby

Secrets from Grandma's Attic is a trademark of Guideposts.

Published by Guideposts Books & Inspirational Media
100 Reserve Road, Suite E200
Danbury, CT 06810
Guideposts.org

Copyright © 2023 by Guideposts. All rights reserved.

This book, or parts thereof, may not be reproduced, stored in a retrieval system, or transmitted in any form or by any means, electronic, mechanical, photocopying, recording, or otherwise, without the written permission of the publisher.

This is a work of fiction. While the setting of Secrets from Grandma's Attic as presented in this series is fictional, the location of Canton, Missouri, actually exists, and some places and characters may be based on actual places and people whose identities have been used with permission or fictionalized to protect their privacy. Apart from the actual people, events, and locales that figure into the fiction narrative, all other names, characters, businesses, and events are the creation of the author's imagination and any resemblance to actual persons or events is coincidental.

Every attempt has been made to credit the sources of copyrighted material used in this book. If any such acknowledgment has been inadvertently omitted or miscredited, receipt of such information would be appreciated.

Scripture references are from the following sources: *The Holy Bible, King James Version* (KJV). *The Holy Bible, New International Version* (NIV). Copyright © 1973, 1978, 1984, 2011 by Biblica, Inc. Used by permission of Zondervan. All rights reserved worldwide. www.zondervan.com

Cover and interior design by Müllerhaus
Cover illustration by Greg Copeland at Illustration Online LLC.
Typeset by Aptara, Inc.

ISBN 978-1-959634-49-2 (hardcover)
ISBN 978-1-959634-55-3 (epub)

Printed and bound in the United States of America
10 9 8 7 6 5 4 3 2 1

Nothing Gold Can Stay

Chapter One

*E*leven-year-old Matt set his Swashbuckler Burger down and wiped off a string of melted cheese that looped from his bottom lip. "Arrr," he said, voice low and pirate-ish. "'Many's the long night I've dreamed of cheese—toasted, mostly.'"

Amy Allen laughed at the antics of the boy sitting across from her. He'd been reading *Treasure Island* and memorizing lines from the book for the past two weeks, inspiring her choice of restaurants for their celebration. "Glad you're enjoying it, matey."

Jana, aged seven, sighed as she dipped a chicken "gold nugget" into ranch dressing. "This tastes as good as having a puppy."

Amy laughed and wrapped an arm around her. "Not this again."

Jana responded with a pout accompanied by melodramatic, pleading eyes. "If we can't have a puppy, can we please, please, please get the Shipwreck Sundae?"

Saying no to those adorable eyes was one of the hardest things Amy had learned to do since Matt and Jana entered her life. They were here to celebrate two years since they'd come to live with her as foster children. Their adoption had been finalized eight months ago, and she was still getting used to the fact that she no longer needed to fear that someone would take them away from her. Since National Adoption Day was in November, she had some special plans for their family's Thanksgiving gathering later in the month, but tonight was just for the three of them. And tonight was not a night for saying no. Except, maybe, to getting a puppy. "You bet. We can each choose two scoops and two toppings."

As her children cheered, Amy sipped her mango smoothie and looked around the restaurant. River Dan's, built on the Mississippi River in Quincy, Illinois, had opened a month ago, but this was their first visit. The interior appeared so authentic she could almost imagine them rocking back and forth with the movement of the ship. Their table was made of wide, distressed planks. Shiplap walls drew the eye upward to a low ceiling where light fixtures that looked like oil lamps hung every few feet. Heavy iron chains, thick ropes, and old, weathered tackle hung from iron hooks. A doorway led to a large banquet room labeled CAPTAIN'S TABLE. The kid-friendly menu offered dishes with seaworthy names like Sailor's Stew, Frigate Fries, and Pirate Pizza. "Think we should come back here sometime?" she asked.

"Definitely." Matt gave a ketchup-covered thumbs-up.

Jana nodded emphatically. "Can we bring Natalie and Colton next time we—" She stopped and sighed when Amy's phone, sitting between them, vibrated.

Amy smiled at the name on her screen. Sara Willey, Amy's niece and the other first-grade teacher at Canton Elementary, had recently become her biggest cheerleader for the online business she was starting. Amy answered with an enthusiastic "Hi!"

"Are you in the middle of something? I've got some ideas to run by you."

"I'm out for dinner with the kids. Can you give me the highlights?"

"I'll talk fast. I thought of a new idea for you to expand your market. What if, instead of offering printables just for teachers, you also made some for parents? Chore lists, menu planners, encouraging notes for moms to put in backpacks and lunch boxes, things like that."

"I love it," Amy said. Sara, mom to two toddlers, knew what she was talking about. "I've learned so many parenting hacks in the past two years. If I stick to my theme of making it all fun… Wow. The sky's the limit." Amy took a bite of a frigate fry as her own ideas began to fall like leaves from the trees along the river.

"I wonder if you could…" As Sara rattled off several more ideas, Amy became aware of a strange, hushed conversation taking place at her table.

"Dill pickle ice cream with anchovies and hot sauce," Matt whispered.

"Frozen yogurt with swiss cheese and chocolate sprinkles," Jana countered.

"Pepperoni and broccoli on liver ice cream with blue cheese on the side." Matt's voice rose above a whisper.

Suppressing a laugh, Amy said, "Sara, I love your ideas. Let's talk tomorrow, okay?" She ended the call and set her phone on the table. "At least I never have to worry about you two getting bored. You bring the entertainment with you."

They chatted about school and what they'd do over Christmas break while they finished eating. Matt cleaned his plate, but Jana pushed aside two of her chicken nuggets and some fries, saying she wanted to take them home for breakfast the next day.

"I suppose you're too full for a Shipwreck Sundae then."

"No way."

Amy laughed and motioned to their server. She let Jana order first, hoping "frozen yogurt with swiss cheese" wouldn't be the first words out of her mouth.

When their order arrived, Matt gasped, Jana clapped, and Amy groaned as she took a few pictures of the sundae that came in a plastic pirate's ship with three long-handled gold spoons. The ship's hold cradled their selected combo of butter pecan, Mississippi Mud, strawberry, Moose Tracks, Peanut Butter Explosion, and Zanzibar Chocolate topped with hot fudge, salted caramel, marshmallow cream, peanuts, chocolate chips, and rainbow sprinkles. Whipped cream and three maraschino cherries completed the concoction, as if it needed more.

"Best day ever, Mom," Matt said as they exited the booth twenty minutes later.

"Mine too," Jana chimed in.

"Best kids ever." Amy hugged them both and then dropped her arms when her phone dinged with a text. Niesha, her website designer. She swiped to read the message.

I SENT YOU A COUPLE OF LOGO OPTIONS I'D LIKE YOU TO LOOK AT.

"Wonderful." She opened the attachment, and when she raised her eyes to see where the kids were, her steps slowed. She squinted at the weathered and splintered board tacked to the shiplap above the front door. Splotches of reddish varnish hinted that it had once sported a polished finish. Letters, carved or routered, black paint peeling, spelled out RIVER DAN. Was this old piece of wood the inspiration for the restaurant's name? But that wasn't the question that blared in her mind. The words, the cursive font... She'd seen them before, in a photograph in her grandmother's attic. Were the words *River Dan* part of something longer? Her pulse skipped a beat.

She wouldn't know for sure until she talked to her aunt, but she had a feeling this piece of wood was only part of what it once was.

Amy waited while the hostess sat two parties of four. When the young woman returned, Amy pointed to the sign above the door. "Can you tell me anything about that board? Do you know where it was found or its history?"

"History?" A confused, blank stare accompanied the single word.

"Is the owner or manager here?"

"I think he's in his office." She smiled at two silver-haired ladies walking in. "Two? Table or booth?" She picked up menus and led them into the dining room.

Amy sighed, loud and exasperated enough that Jana looked up at her with surprise.

"She could have at least—" Amy cut off her rant. The kids didn't need her poor example of how to handle frustration. But the hostess could have pointed the way to the manager's office. "Let's go. I'll call tomorrow."

When they were in the car, Matt began peppering her with questions. "Why were you asking about that old board? Who's River Dan? Do you know him?"

"Why were you mad at that lady?" Jana asked.

Amy took a slow, calming breath. She wouldn't normally react like that. It was a Friday night, and the restaurant was busy. Her normal self would have cut the woman some slack. But this week, with getting ready to open her Etsy store, working with the web designer, and trying to create enough marketable content to start a viable business on top of teaching and helping Carrie Ellis with a fundraiser for Pop's Place, a home for single moms, she was stretched to her emotional limit. She managed a wobbly smile in the rearview mirror. "I shouldn't have gotten upset with her. I asked a question, and I was hoping for an answer, but... Anyway"—she widened her tired smile—"how would you two like to stop in and see Aunt Ruth and Uncle Marvin for a bit?"

The question was answered with a cheer in stereo.

Matt sang one of his made-up pirate songs as they drove north on Highway 61. When Amy slowed the car in front of the ranch house with the red front door, she wished she'd called first. Though her aunt and uncle had an open-door policy, and she knew she was always welcome, she'd be interrupting something, if only a television show. Interrupting with what Aunt Ruth would probably prove was a crazy question. Tracy, Amy's big sister, had always teased her about "imaginating" too much. This was likely a case in point. The restaurant owner was probably named Dan. They'd probably found an old board and painted "River Dan" on it.

They walked up the sidewalk that had been lined with hydrangeas, geraniums, and pansies over the summer. A few hardy orange and yellow mums still held wilting blooms, now buffeted by the crisp November wind.

Uncle Marvin greeted them at the door with hugs. Aunt Ruth was sitting in the living room, a quilt-in-progress draped over her lap. "Come in," she called. "What a fun surprise. What can we get you? Soda? Coffee? Tea?"

"We're good. We just had dinner." Amy took the chair closest to Aunt Ruth, and the kids sat on the love seat.

Uncle Marvin said, "There's always room for a snickerdoodle, right?"

"How about one to take home?" Amy answered, then described their dessert.

Uncle Marvin laughed. "Cookies on top of a Shipwreck Sundae sounds like a recipe for a shipwrecked night. I'll put some in a bag."

He headed for the kitchen, and Amy pulled out her phone. "I have something to show you." She swiped to the picture she'd taken and handed the phone to Aunt Ruth. She'd decided to keep her speculations to herself and wait for Aunt Ruth's reaction.

Her aunt's eyes widened. "What... Where... Where did you take this?"

Amy told her about River Dan's.

"This is from the name board from *River Dancer.*"

Goose bumps skittered down Amy's arms. "How can you be sure?"

"Look." Aunt Ruth enlarged the picture, and Amy bent closer. "See the scratches under the words? Not long before it disappeared, I got in the biggest trouble of my entire young life. I carved our initials—R, A, and N."

Amy gasped at the letters that hadn't been discernable from a distance. "Ruth, Abigail, and Noah."

"Yes."

"So this really is a piece of *River Dancer.*"

"Beyond the shadow of a doubt."

"Disappeared?" Matt's eyes were as big and round as Oreos.

Aunt Ruth nodded. "Get comfy, and I'll tell you the story."

Jana pulled a lap quilt out of a basket next to the love seat and curled up with her feet under her. Matt, on the other hand, slid off the couch and settled cross-legged at Aunt Ruth's feet.

"Way back in the olden days in the 1950s, when Great-aunt Abigail, your mom's father, and I were little, our parents, Grandpa Howard and Grandma Pearl, owned a boat named *River Dancer*."

Matt leaned forward. "Like a rowboat or a big, huge boat?"

Amy jumped in to help give some perspective. "If I remember right, in the picture I saw, it was probably a bit bigger than Colton and Natalie's speed boat." Why did she avoid saying their father's name? Maybe because her brain still scrambled just a bit every time she thought about Dr. Miles Anderson with the coffee-with-a-splash-of-cream eyes—and their second chance at romance.

"It had a cabin that was big enough for all three of us kids to take a nap in," Aunt Ruth said. "Anyway, in the spring of 1955, we had a college girl living with us. One day she just disappeared."

Matt's eyebrows rose. "Like poof? Like aliens abducted her?"

"Not quite so dramatic. We woke up one morning and she was gone. And so was the boat."

"That's scary." Jana's eyes were wide.

"Nothing scary, honey." Aunt Ruth opened her arms. Amy's heart warmed when Jana went to sit on her aunt's lap. "My parents said they thought she probably went to live with a friend of hers." Aunt Ruth locked eyes with Amy. Her gaze said there was much more to this story.

"So if it wasn't aliens," Matt said, "maybe it was pirates. I read that they used to hide in caves along the river. Maybe there are underground tunnels and a whole pirate civilization lived underground for like a hundred years after everybody thought they were gone. I bet they climbed up a trellis and stole the girl and then the boat and she's still living in the tunnels.

"There were girl pirates, you know. I read about a girl named Anne Bonny who fell in love with a buccaneer named Calico Jack. She could shoot a pistol and use a cutlass just like Calico Jack's crew, and she and Cora Read, another girl pirate, raided a bunch of boats and took their booty, but then their ship was captured by a band of pirate-hunters. Calico Jack and some of his men were hung, but they let Anne Bonny and Cora Read live 'cause they were going to have babies."

Amy cringed. *Note to self: Pre-read the books the boy checks out of the library.*

"Well, that certainly is a theory." Aunt Ruth pressed her lips together, holding back a smile. "We'll keep pirates in mind while we try to figure out how that board got to the restaurant."

Matt grinned. "Awesome. Mom, we need your notebook. Aunt Ruth, tell us everything you know about the girl who disappeared. We're gonna solve this mystery."

Chapter Two

Amy handed her notebook and a pen to Matt. "The hostess at River Dan's couldn't give me any information. I'm going to try to talk to the owner or manager tomorrow." She pointed at the phone, still in Ruth's hand. "How old were you when you carved your names, and how did you do it?"

"I was seven, old enough to know better. Dad special-ordered the name board, and it was sitting on the table while he looked for the right screws to mount it on the stern. I was learning cursive, and I decided to surprise him by copying the pretty lettering and adding our names. With a fork." Aunt Ruth grimaced.

Jana gasped. "Did you get in so much trouble?"

Aunt Ruth nodded. "I'd never seen my father so angry." As she stared at the picture of the old, weathered board, she seemed to be revisiting the emotions of that day. "But your mom's grandpa had a big, soft heart that never let him stay mad very long. After a miserable day, he gave me a long lecture and said he wasn't going to sand out the names because, even though I was wrong to do it, it was our boat too, and our names should be on it."

"That was nice." Jana nestled against Aunt Ruth's shoulder.

"How long did you have the boat before it went missing?" Amy asked.

"A year. It, and Violet, disappeared halfway through our second summer with *River Dancer*. I've searched for information about both of them. I was sure that with the ability to find people online I could finally discover what happened to her. I've looked up her and her fiancé's names, checked obituaries and social media and newspaper archives, but never found a thing. I think my mother knew more than she was willing to tell us about what happened that night. I've wondered over the years if she was protecting Violet or just didn't want to taint her memory in our minds." Aunt Ruth smiled. "Abigail will be here around four tomorrow afternoon. I can't wait to tell her about this. She only has vague memories of Violet, but she may have heard things I didn't. She had a different relationship with Mom than I did."

"They definitely shared the same sense of humor."

"Oh yes." Aunt Ruth laughed. "And I think because Abigail never married, she confided more in Mom. After Dad died, I think that camaraderie went both ways."

"I suppose you've already called her today."

"Woke her up to wish her a happy birthday at five forty-five this morning." Aunt Ruth grinned. "So glad I was born in the afternoon. Anyway, I don't think I'll tell her over the phone. Maybe I'll wait until Sunday when we're all together. We can tell everyone about this, and then we'll see what she knows."

"Violet was your nanny, right?"

"Yes. She'd been our babysitter for years, probably since I was born, so she was already practically part of the family. We must have been five, seven, and eight when she came to live with us. Now that you have children, you can imagine what a huge help that was to your grandma when she was a young mom. Though, looking back, I'm sure my parents invited her to stay with us because her father had just passed away and she didn't have any other family. Her mother had left them years earlier, and the poor girl was all alone in a huge empty house."

"Sounds like it was a good arrangement for everyone."

Aunt Ruth nodded. "We had so much fun with her. She was a storyteller. Instead of reading books to us before bed, she'd make up long, tall tales. I also figured out much later that she wove real historical events into her stories. She was a history major, and I think she might have been using us to help cement details she needed to remember."

"Do you think she stole the boat?"

"I don't know. I remember somebody saying she could have eloped with her boyfriend, but that theory never made sense to me. Violet was engaged. I remember staring at her diamond in the sunshine when we went on a picnic. She had a photograph album full of pictures she'd cut from magazines. Bridal gowns and flowers and cakes. I loved paging through it. She asked Abigail and me to be flower girls. She'd already made our dresses, and several women helped sew hers. There were so many pearls, all sewn on by hand. It was beautiful. It made no sense that she'd suddenly run off and get married. And why take the boat?"

Aunt Ruth sighed. "Plus, I have this vague memory of her fiancé having a hushed conversation with my father in his study, and I'm sure it was after Violet disappeared because I was trying to listen in to find out if she was coming back." She rubbed her temple. "I wish I could remember more. The whole thing just feels like unfinished business. Like a puzzle with a piece missing."

Nothing Gold Can Stay

"I get that," Amy said. "Maybe now we've got a clue to finding that last piece."

"Maybe."

Amy had never thought of Aunt Ruth as old. Although she was just weeks away from her seventy-seventh birthday, she still had her quick wit and faced aging with what Amy viewed as a perfect balance between embracing and resisting. But she had recently lost a close friend from church, and at this moment there was a weariness in her eyes. Would solving this mystery be a healthy distraction? "Who were Grandma and Grandpa's close friends back then? Are any of them still alive?"

Aunt Ruth's brow furrowed. "The Popelstopps. Mom and Dad used to play canasta with Pop and his wife. And there was a couple from church they mentored for years. The Pasternaks, Katerina and Silva. Violet was in their wedding while she was living with us. They're in their upper eighties now, still living in a big old farmhouse out on Highway P. I try to get out to see them every couple of months. Otherwise, everyone's gone."

"That gives us a place to start. Tomorrow morning I'll call the owner of River Dan's. It'll be easy to talk to Pop anytime, since he's living at Harbor House. Do you think the Pasternaks would be open to us visiting?"

"Us?" Matt grinned. "Me too?"

"I don't want to go," Jana said.

"That's okay. I bet Olivia would love to come and spend time with you." Amy turned to Aunt Ruth. "What do you think? Can the Pasternaks handle an eleven-year-old who thinks he's a pirate?"

Instead of the affirmation Amy expected, Aunt Ruth's face seemed to tighten with apprehension. "I think we need to be a bit…

cautious. It's true that 1955 was a very long time ago, but there may still be those who want their secrets kept buried." Aunt Ruth ran her finger along a feather-stitched seam of the quilt she'd laid on the end table next to her. "While I was eavesdropping on the conversation Violet's fiancé had with my father, I heard one thing very clearly. As he was walking out the door, he said, 'That could prove to be very dangerous.'"

Saturday dawned with clear blue skies and very little wind, making the words 'That could prove to be very dangerous' seem like something Amy had heard in a movie. Aunt Ruth's comment that some may still be alive who wanted to keep their secrets buried had infiltrated her dreams. But her first cup of coffee and her prayer time had dispelled all sense of trepidation and allowed her to give in to Matt's request to go along when she and Aunt Ruth visited the Pasternaks. He had plans with Miles's son Colton at ten, but at least he'd get in on some of the day's mystery solving.

After giving instructions to Olivia, their sitter, and hugging Jana, Amy left the house with the enthusiasm and anticipation of a mountain climber setting out on an expedition.

Aunt Ruth stepped out of her house, carrying a square-bottomed bag. "I went over to Tracy's last night and found this in the attic." She pulled out a photograph in a gold filigree frame.

A click sounded in the back seat, and Matt leaned over Amy's shoulder. Aunt Ruth patted his arm. "Glad we have our super sleuth with us. We might need your skills today."

Amy studied the photo of a shiny wood boat with a gleaming brass bell. On a board fastened to the stern, in rounded black script, were the words "River Dancer."

"Whoa," Matt exclaimed. "That's the ghost ship?"

Aunt Ruth laughed. "How many times have you seen *Pirates of the Caribbean*?"

"Only three." His smile was evident in his voice.

Matt sat back and refastened his seat belt, and Amy drove out of the driveway.

"I will admit this picture made me a little sad after seeing what the wood on that board looks like now," Auth Ruth said. "Dad spent hours waxing what he called his pride and joy. I remember Mom teasing him that she was jealous and Dad saying that would keep her on her toes. All I could picture was ballet toe shoes." Aunt Ruth smiled and then sighed. She took a plastic container out of the bag. "I figured blueberry muffins might help this morning."

"We need blueberry muffin help?" Amy made her voice squeak just a tad with faux fear. "Who are these people anyway?"

"Oh, you're in for a treat. Katerina is… Well, you've watched *I Love Lucy* reruns, right?"

Amy pictured the comical redheaded TV star from the fifties and sixties. "Not for years, but I think I get the picture. She's a Lucy?"

"Yep. I used to try not to laugh, but I think she actually enjoys entertaining people with her antics."

"I just hope she remembers something that will help."

When Aunt Ruth pointed at a driveway leading uphill to a white Victorian with a wraparound porch and a matching gazebo, Amy's breath hitched. "*This* house?"

"You've been here?"

"Oh yes. Grandma Pearl brought us here several times. Did you ever hear the story of Tracy and me and the cinnamon applesauce?"

"That was Katerina?" Aunt Ruth's eyes grew wide with mirth. "Why am I not surprised?"

"I felt so bad...after Grandma rushed us to the bathroom so we could spit and spit and wash out our mouths. Mrs. Pasternak was so proud of her homemade applesauce. I remember her saying, 'It started with C, and who can tell the difference between cinnamon and cayenne anyway?'"

"Ew," Matt said from the back seat.

Aunt Ruth echoed Matt's reaction. "Well, now you know why I brought food."

At least a dozen chickens scattered as Amy drove up the gravel drive. "The names Katerina and Silva don't sound familiar though."

"Grandma called them Sil and Rina, but I love their old-world names."

They walked up three steps to a door with a sign that read, DON'T BOTHER KNOCKING, WE CAN'T HEAR YOU ANYWAY.

"Oh boy." Amy laughed and stepped into an enclosed porch. As Aunt Ruth raised her hand to knock on the inside door, it swung open, and a trim woman about Amy's height with deep smile lines and red hair greeted them. "Ruthy and Amy!" she shouted. "And... is this handsome young man yours, Amy? Come in, come in. Don't mind the mess. I'm reorganizing the pantry." She sounded like she was yelling to someone out in the barn behind the house.

"Hearing aid!" The deep voice came from somewhere beyond the kitchen.

"Searing pain?" The color drained from Katerina's face as she shouted back. "What did you do to yourself now?" She turned and took a step then grabbed the corner of the kitchen counter for support. "Sil? What hurts?"

Aunt Ruth rested a hand on her arm. "I think he was just reminding you to put in your hearing aids," she said, gently but loudly.

"Well, fiddledeedee. That's all he's mumbling about? Thought he'd cut off his hand or something." Katerina walked over to an open cupboard and took out a small box.

Amy used the time to look around. Every square inch of kitchen counter was crammed with jars, boxes, and bags. The packaging on several items made it clear they hadn't been bought in the present millennium. She scanned a row of small red-and-white shaker cans, sure she'd find the offending cayenne from four decades ago in the lineup.

Aunt Ruth handed Katerina the muffins. "Thought you might like a Saturday morning treat."

"What a godsend," Katerina exclaimed. "Poor Sil has been grumbling since daybreak about not having a decent breakfast for a week." She gestured at the avocado-green electric stove, its burners almost completely obscured by cereal boxes. One, a blue Honey Frosted Wheaties box, bore a picture of a grinning Tiger Woods holding a massive trophy. Below his name were the words, "Our Newest Champion." Amy cringed. That box was from the late nineties. She thought of the number of times she'd told the kids to never set anything flammable on their glass cooktop and forced herself to look away.

"Would you like some help with this?" she asked. It was the teacher in her that loved organizing and couldn't think straight in the midst of a mess. She had shown restraint by not saying, "Would you like some help getting rid of this stuff?"

"That's so sweet of you, but no. I'm making labels and putting everything back in categories."

Amy conceded. They'd lived into their eighties without paying attention to expiration dates. It wasn't her place to swoop in and try to save them from old food—or fire.

Silva was sitting in a leather recliner in what must at one time have been called the parlor. His bald head reflected light from the floor lamp next to the chair. He jumped up when they walked in. "Welcome." He held out his hand to Matt, who introduced himself. "Nice to meet you, Matt. Ruth, it's so good to see you. And can this possibly be little Amy, one of the girls my wife tried to poison?" His deep laugh rumbled in his chest as he pulled them both into a hug.

"After all these years, you'd think you could let that ball drop. It wasn't my fault, anyway, it was the lettering on the can." Katerina gestured to the chairs that surrounded a round, low table. "I'll get coffee."

"Can I help?" Aunt Ruth asked.

Katerina shook her head. "You just get comfy." She left the room, and Amy and Aunt Ruth settled in comfortable chairs covered in red and gold brocade. Matt sat on a straight-back chair with a small braided rug serving as a cushion.

"Your home is so beautiful," Amy said. "It made me think of a castle on a hill when I was little."

"Thank you. My grandparents built it in 1907." Silva rested his elbows on his knees. Wearing a long-sleeved blue shirt with the cuffs folded back, he looked like a man who still worked hard. His white beard was trimmed close. After removing wire-rimmed glasses, he tented his fingers. "Rina tells me you're here to ask about Violet Conway and Howard and Pearl's boat."

"Yes," Amy said. "We think we've found a piece of the boat."

His eyes flashed in surprise. "Where did you find it?"

She told him about the restaurant, watching his face as she did.

"But that's all? Just a piece from the stern?"

"That's all we know about. We're going to talk to the restaurant owner later this morning."

Katerina returned, a white carafe in one hand. In the other, she clutched a cluster of four brightly colored mugs like a bouquet of spring flowers. A small plastic bottle was tucked under her arm. "Coffee all around? Chocolate milk for the young man?"

Amy and Aunt Ruth nodded in tandem. Amy prayed the expiration date on the chocolate milk hadn't passed by too much.

With surprisingly steady movements, Katerina filled the mugs. "So, Amy, you're the teacher, right? And your sister works for the paper. And you've got two children? Your grandmother was so proud of you girls. Did you know your grandparents were our mentors? They met with us for years. Helped us through the painful time of realizing we'd never have children and—"

"Rina." Silva held out a hand, palm down, and slowly lowered it.

Katerina sank into a chair like a deflating balloon. "You think you saw a piece of the boat, but you don't know where it was found?"

"Right." Aunt Ruth turned to Silva. "What do you remember about Vi's disappearance?"

"Very little. There wasn't much to remember, because we just didn't know anything. We had our own theories, of course, but never any proof. The last we heard was that a professor at the college received a telegram a couple of months after Violet went missing. No idea who it was from, but it said something to the effect that we should call off the search for Vi, the boat, and the treasure."

"Treasure?" Again, Amy and Aunt Ruth spoke in tandem, but Matt's voice carried above theirs. "What treasure? *Real* treasure?"

Their hosts reacted with the same expression of surprise. "You don't know about the map?" Katerina asked.

"What map?" Amy set her mug down.

Silva and Katerina shared a look. Silva cleared his throat. "We don't know if Violet ran away or someone abducted her, but however it happened, it was all because of a map she found in her father's home office after he died. A pirate treasure map."

Chapter Three

Katerina set a muffin on a small plate and handed it to Silva. "The map could have been centuries old, one of our professors said. It was drawn on deer skin, probably with ink made from black walnuts. It showed the islands just south of here, and there were numbers and arrows on them leading to Teal Island."

"There's nothing on Teal Island," Matt said. "Remember, Mom? Dr. Miles took us out there."

Amy nodded. Miles had taken her and the kids out on the river a week ago. They'd passed Willow, Teal, and Hogback Islands, all part of the Great River National Wildlife Refuge. Tiny Teal Island was densely wooded with only one narrow sandy beach on the southwest side. "It's possible it looked very different almost seventy years ago."

How would Violet's father have gotten ahold of an old treasure map? "Is there anything else you can tell us?"

"Any little detail might help," Aunt Ruth added. "Do you think the telegram could have been from Violet?"

Katerina shrugged. "I hated to think that was a possibility, but she was so distraught after her father passed. She couldn't stand being in that big old house alone. That was why she moved in with your family. Going through her father's things was so hard for her. It's possible she had some kind of mental breakdown and just wasn't the sweet Violet we knew. Maybe she developed multiple personality disorder and had an alter ego that her real self didn't even know about. Like in that movie about—"

"Rina."

Once again, Silva's gentle but no-nonsense voice seemed to snap Katerina out of her version of imagining.

"Like Rina said, she was the sweetest person, but grief can do strange things. We all loved Vi," he said, "but there was no denying that she was spoiled and accustomed to getting her own way."

Katerina pinched off a bit of muffin and nodded her agreement. "Vi was used to nice things. Her mother ran off and left them when she was just a little girl, and her father tried to compensate by making Vi his little princess. Anything she wanted, she got. New car, European vacations every summer. We heard rumors that all that spoiling had left her father with very little savings. We wondered if discovering she was an orphan with limited funds terrified her. Maybe enough to do something desperate like steal a boat and go hunting for treasure."

"Without us." Silva patted Katerina's arm. "We had a plan to look for it together. There were six of us. Vi, and Lenny Therwood, her fiancé, Rina and me, and Don Kennedy and his girlfriend, Ellen. We were all close friends from school. We'd made a pact not to tell anyone, and we all promised we wouldn't go looking for the treasure on our own."

"So you all saw the map?"

Silva nodded. "Oh, and we showed it to Professor Janvier."

Katerina flattened her hand against her chest. "Antoine Janvier was from Paris. He was wounded in World War II. An American army nurse tended him, and they fell madly in love. She wanted to be close to her family back in the States, so he left Paris to marry her. All of us girls thought it was the most romantic story, but you didn't have to spend much time around the two of them to see it was all a facade. Whatever love they'd once had must have faded. I remember one day when she—"

"Rina." Silva touched her shoulder with tenderness. "Let's save their story for a bit later." He turned to Amy and Aunt Ruth. "Antoine Janvier and William Conway, Violet's father, had been friends for years. Janvier took Conway's place as head of the history department. He's the one who confirmed the map was authentic."

"Violet showed the map to Pearl first," Katerina said. "Too many eyes on the prize, if you ask me. Loose lips sink ships, they say. I think loose lips also give clues to treasure from sunken ships."

Matt's eyes widened. "The treasure was from a sunken pirate ship?"

Katerina's thin shoulders rose. "More likely it came from a merchant ship that was boarded by pirates and then sunk. Piracy on the upper Mississippi started after the Revolutionary War. There were huge gangs that wrecked havoc, especially around St. Louis and Cairo. It lasted about forty years. In the late 1700s, Stack Island was crawling with river pirates and counterfeiters."

Amy smiled at Katerina's word mix-up. But *"wrecked* havoc" was probably a more accurate way to describe pirate activity on the river anyway. "You've done your research."

Silva darted a glance at his wife. Amy watched their wordless communication with wonder. She and Miles were beginning to share moments like that. What would it be like to have decades together to hone those skills? With effort, she focused back on Silva's answer. "...tried to find her. Rina and I had started exploring the islands, hoping to find something that would tell us what happened to Vi and the boat."

"Until they told us to stop." Katerina clasped her fingers in her lap, as if restraining some inner emotion.

"Which professor was the telegram sent to?" Amy asked.

"Professor Janvier," Silva told her. "It said, 'Tell your lackeys to call off the search for Violet or someone will get hurt.'"

"'Lackeys'?" Amy looked from Katerina to Silva. "They actually used that word?"

Silva nodded. "Sounded like something right out of an Edward G. Robinson movie."

"It was enough to scare us," Katerina added.

Aunt Ruth set her mug on the table and sat up ramrod straight. "I was only eight at the time, but I overheard a conversation between my father and Lenny. All I remember was him telling my father that something could be very dangerous."

Silva took a sip of coffee and gave a slow nod. "Professor Janvier showed the telegram to the police. A few days later, two officers came to our apartment and told us to drop our search because we were putting ourselves in danger. They made it sound like they were worried about us exploring the islands because of all the marshy areas. I remember one of them saying the islands were basically unexplored wildernesses and there could be quicksand or poisonous snakes, but we knew they were really trying to get us to stop because there was something even more dangerous than anything we'd find in nature."

"You can guess how our imaginations sprouted wings." Katerina's hands fluttered like a bird in flight. "Maybe the mob, or escaped convicts. Just a few months earlier there'd been huge prison riots in New Jersey and Michigan, and we watched the coverage on the news. That fed our wild ideas. We even wondered if there were still pirates living on the islands."

Amy had a hard time not grinning at the look of astonishment on her son's face. "Did you ever find out what the danger was?"

"No." Silva wrapped his hands around his mug.

"And Lenny never heard from Violet?"

"Not that we know of," Katerina said. "He just up and left right after she disappeared. He told us he couldn't stand being here in town with all the memories of her. We never heard a word from him."

"What about Don and Ellen?" Amy asked.

Silva stared out the window as if gazing into the past. "They broke up right around that time. Ellen married about a year later. She lives in St. Louis. Don wasn't around when we found out Vi had disappeared. Visiting his grandmother, I think. When he came back, he was different. He was always the life of the party, the one who made all the plans for our little group. Funny guy, always making jokes and pulling pranks, but after Vi went missing, he was... sober, I guess you'd say. He kept to himself and wasn't even interested in helping us search the islands. And then he left."

Katerina sighed. "We never did know where he went, but we heard not long ago he moved back to Canton. Guess it's just too painful for him to come see us." She looked at Silva, who nodded, and then she turned to Amy. "Don had a half brother living here in town. We didn't think of it at the time, but now we suspect he had some mental health issues, as they say today. Anyway, he and Don were always at odds. The brother died a few months ago. I think that's why Don and his wife decided to move back to Canton. Or maybe Don left town for the same reason Lenny did. Because he was sweet on Vi."

"Rina."

"Well, it's true. And maybe it's relevant. Maybe he told her how he felt and she left to get away from him."

Aunt Ruth stood in front of the weathered board above River Dan's entrance. A wistful look shimmered in her eyes. "It's like...reconnecting. I remember the day Dad bought *River Dancer*. We all waited at the marina wearing brand-new life jackets. Your father would have been five at the time. He and Abigail held hands and jumped up and down on the dock yelling, 'A boat! A boat! A real boat!' I was the mature one, at eight. I remember trying to copy my mother's posture, folding my hands and calmly waiting. But then *River Dancer* came into view, every surface shining in the sunlight. Dad rang the brass bell, and I couldn't help acting wild and crazy like the others."

Amy had seen pictures of her father as a little boy. A towhead, with bright blue eyes. How he would have enjoyed this moment. Twenty-six years had passed since the accident that took both of her parents, but there were still moments—holidays, birthdays, Matt and Jana's adoption party—when she missed them as if it were yesterday. She breathed through the pang of grief in her chest and focused on her father's sister and the sentiments that must be roiling in her mind. She slid an arm across Aunt Ruth's shoulder. "Maybe this is the first step in giving you some closure."

"I hope so." Aunt Ruth took a shaky breath. "That day, before any of us got on the boat, Mom prayed over it, asking God to bless and protect us and every person who set foot on *River Dancer*. She prayed that same prayer every time we went out, no matter who was with us. I've wondered if her faith was shaken after it disappeared, presumably with Violet on it."

"Such a mystery," Amy said. "I bet Grandma wrote about it in her diary."

"I'm sure she did." Aunt Ruth tapped one finger on her chin. "And I'm pretty sure Dad saved a newspaper article about it."

Amy smiled. "He saved everything else." Amy's grandparents were notorious for keeping anything that might be of value or interest in the future. That future was now, and their daughter and three granddaughters were the ones charged with deciding what was valuable or interesting and what needed to be trashed, saved, or donated.

The same hostess that had given Amy no help the day before stepped through a door camouflaged by seashells and hanging fish nets. "Mr. Jordan will be with you in a moment. Please come with me."

As they wove around empty tables, Aunt Ruth whispered, "I love this place." When the hostess stopped at a back booth, Amy thanked her and sat down. Aunt Ruth turned in a slow circle, taking in the ambiance. "I half expect to see water out those portholes." She sat next to Amy and ran her hand across the marred surface of the table. "If their food is as good as you say it is, I may have to bring your uncle here for dinner."

"He would love it." Amy listened to muffled voices coming from the kitchen. The restaurant would open in an hour. "Strange to be here when it's so quiet." She spoke in a hushed tone. The silence seemed to require it.

Footsteps echoed off the shiplap, and Amy turned to see a man who appeared to be in his forties walking toward them. Black hair with a closely trimmed beard, black button-down shirt, black pants. He could well be descended from the pirates that once hid in the coves along the river.

The man held out his hand to Aunt Ruth as he lowered himself into the booth across from her. "Welcome to River Dan's. I'm Dan Jordan."

Aunt Ruth and Amy introduced themselves, and then Amy said, "My children and I had a delicious dinner here last night. As we were leaving, I recognized the 'River Dan' board you have nailed over the entryway."

"You recognized it?"

Amy motioned to Aunt Ruth to finish the story.

"It's from the back of a boat that was stolen from my parents in 1955."

"St-stolen?" Dan Jordan appeared ready to jump out of his seat in excitement. "That's...wow. You're sure?"

"Yes. I carved the letters beneath the words when I was eight. The boat was called *River Dancer*."

"Seriously?" Dan rubbed his arm. "I never get goose bumps, but this... Wow. Where was it stolen from?"

"Our boat slip in Canton. Our nanny disappeared at the same time."

"Oh. Man. Do you know what happened to her? Did she take the boat, or...?"

"We have as many questions as you do," Aunt Ruth answered.

"Where did you get the board?" Amy asked.

"My son Josh and some of his buddies kayaked down near John Hay Recreation Area a few years ago. Josh tipped his kayak when the current pushed him into a tangle of roots, and after he righted it, he found that board. The tree had actually grown around it, so it had to have been in that spot for years. Decades, probably. Josh has pictures. He gave me the board as a joke for Father's Day. I'd just sold a restaurant up in Rochester, Minnesota. We moved to Quincy to help care for my wife's parents, and I was starting to scout out locations for a new venue. That board was the inspiration. My son handed it to me and said, 'It's a sign, Dad. Literally.'"

Amy laughed. "We'd love to see the pictures and talk to your son."

"He's living in St. Louis now. He's a firefighter with crazy hours, but I'll get your contact info and see if we can arrange something."

"Thank you. Anything else you can tell us?"

"Yes." He glanced toward the front of the store where the sign hung. "If you look closely at the right end, right after the *N*, it's clear it was cut with a saw or some kind of blade. I'm a boater myself, and every time I see that piece of wood, I wonder who would do that and why. Was the boat destroyed in a storm or an accident and there was nothing to do but dismantle it? Now, after what you've told me, I have to wonder if it was something more...sinister."

May 16, 1955

I wish I knew how to comfort Violet. She won't eat, can't sleep. I wasn't sure she was going to make it through graduation. She looked like a zombie walking across the stage. It's been three weeks since her father passed, and just this morning she was finally able to start going through his things. I didn't want her to do it alone, so Howard stayed with the kids while Violet and I went to her house. I busied myself cleaning out the refrigerator and stripping beds while she started with her father's study. I was worried she might find correspondence between her parents or mementos of her mother that would upset her, but what she did find turned out to be amazing.

In a bottom drawer, she found a very, very old map. It appears to be drawn on animal skin! I immediately recognized the shapes of some of the islands just south of here. Willow, Teal, and Hogback. There were numbers on the map, in several inlets and on the islands. Violet is going to show it to the professor who took her father's place as head of the history department. I am so excited for her. This could be something big. I'm no expert, but it looks like a treasure map.

Chapter Four

On Sunday afternoon, Amy stood on a chair and taped a mylar HAPPY BIRTHDAY banner across the archway leading from her sister's kitchen to the library. Aunt Abigail would see it the moment she walked in.

From where she stood, Amy could see through the library, where a table was set for the children, and into the living room. Above the green-and-white tiled fireplace hung a painting of Grandma Pearl at fifteen. Her green velvet dress inspired a young Amy, Tracy, and their cousin Robin to call her "Green Girl." A year and a half ago, they'd found the painting at a flea market and spent weeks unraveling the mystery of how it had gotten from this house to a vendor's table in St. Louis. Amy smiled at the painting. Green Girl was right where she belonged once again.

The house was filled with the aromas of homemade baked macaroni and cheese and smoked pork steak. Since Aunt Abigail frequently complained that she couldn't get "real" barbecue and "fixins" in Michigan where she lived, it had become a tradition to serve up her favorites on her birthday. While Tracy put the finishing touches on a four-layer chocolate cake, her husband, Jeff, checked on the inch-thick steaks he'd brined overnight, rubbed with brown sugar and his secret blend of spices, and put in his backyard smoker. "Cherrywood's the trick," he always said.

Cousin Robin, Aunt Ruth's daughter, opened the refrigerator and pulled out the coleslaw she'd brought then turned to Amy. "Not even a hint?"

"Nope. But I can't believe your mom didn't tell you."

"She loves to torture me. All I know is she wanted to wait until Aunt Abigail was...here." Her voice slowed as a loud duet sung by Matt and Kai, Robin's fourteen-year-old son, came from the living room where the boys and Jana tossed a cloth ball to Sadie, Jeff and Tracy's goldendoodle. "Fifteen men on a dead man's chest," they sang. "Yo-ho-ho, and a bottle of—"

"Root beer!" Amy shouted, cutting them off. This had become a game since Matt had started reading *Treasure Island*.

Robin laughed. "Those boys will—"

The back door flew open with such force Amy almost toppled off the chair. Aunt Abigail, who had turned seventy-six two days ago, burst in, as full of noisy joy as always, followed by Aunt Ruth and Uncle Marvin. "Hello, wonderful family! I come bearing Michigan gifts. But first, hugs." She stepped around the kitchen island and stretched out her arms to Tracy. "Already gave my nephew-in-law a big smacker on his cheek, and now it's your turn." She engulfed Tracy and then turned to Amy. "You're next, toots."

Amy hopped down and was instantly smothered in a hug. "Hope that doctor of yours didn't mind getting a little lipstick on his face."

"He's not..." Before Amy could finish, Aunt Abigail looked past her. "I hear my great-niece and not-so-great nephews in there!"

By the time Jeff brought the pork steaks in, the island was crammed with food and the kitchen was so crowded it was almost impossible to move. Besides people, now numbering twenty, including Tracy's kids and grandkids, the floor and table were strewn with Michigan souvenirs. T-shirts, books, puzzles, six-packs of Vernor's Ginger Ale, and bags of Biggby coffee.

Jeff brought an end to the din by giving a short whistle before saying, "Let's pray." They gathered in a circle around the island and, at Aunt Abigail's suggestion, held hands.

"Lord God, thank You for this bounty of food and for the family You've blessed us with. Help us to honor Aunt Abigail today and show her how much we love her. Amen."

When the children five and up had filled plates and taken seats around the table in the library, the adults and little ones crowded around the dining table where countless dinners had been hosted by Grandma Pearl before she'd "gone home to Glory," as she would say, almost two years ago. Jeff and Tracy had continued the tradition of Sunday dinners, and Amy couldn't be more grateful. It was here, in this house with these people, that the children she now called her own first experienced the true meaning of family.

"Okay, we're all here." Robin looked from Amy to her mother. "What did you find?"

Amy told them about seeing the piece of wood with "River Dan" painted on it then passed her phone around so everyone could see the picture. After that, Aunt Ruth took over, telling about the names she'd scratched into the wood as a child and what they'd learned from Dan Jordan.

Aunt Abigail's eyes grew wide. "That's incredible. If they found this, maybe there's more. Maybe we'll finally find out what happened to Violet."

"So you have no idea?" Amy asked. "Grandma never told you?"

"No," Abigail said. She turned to Aunt Ruth. "Do you think she knew?"

"I don't know," Aunt Ruth said. "I thought Mom might have told you some details I never heard."

Aunt Abigail shook her head. "The only thing I remember is a package arriving not long after Violet disappeared. It was a shiny pink box with a black lid. When Mom opened it, she gasped, and Dad came running. They took it into the pantry, and I overheard them saying it must be from Vi and something about whether or not they should give it to us. Whatever it was, they never did. I asked Mom about it several times over the years and never got a straight answer." Aunt Abigail pointed at the ceiling. "Knowing her, it's probably still up there."

"And we might find some other clues," Aunt Ruth added.

Amy nodded. "Guess we have our after-dinner entertainment figured out."

"I haven't…been up here in forever." Aunt Abigail took a moment to catch her breath after climbing the stairs to the attic. "You've all done a lot of work." Her tone seemed a bit wistful. Did she feel she was missing out? Amy was sure they'd communicated that any time she wanted to make the seven-hour drive from Grand Rapids, her help would be welcome.

"Now that you're here, the real work can begin." Aunt Ruth nudged her sister's shoulder and then walked over to a bank of floor-to-ceiling metal shelves. "I don't think anyone's touched these boxes." She looked to her daughter and nieces for confirmation. Tracy, Amy, and Robin all shook their heads.

"There are still tons of pictures to go through." Amy pointed at a plastic bin where she'd dumped photographs she'd found in dozens of envelopes, shoeboxes, and photo albums. "Grandma was great at writing on the backs but not so good at storing them in order. I've been going through them a little at a time, organizing by year. When we're done, we want to have them all scanned so every member of the family can have digital copies."

"Wonderful." Gaze fixed on the round stained-glass window depicting a single rose in bloom, Aunt Abigail sounded a bit distracted. The attic had that effect on people. Every time Amy stepped into the musty, orange-and-clove-scented space during daylight hours, she had to take a minute to stand and stare at bits of dust floating in shafts of colored light from the window that had been commissioned by her great-grandmother. Each time, she needed a few still moments to filter memories of playing dress-up with Grandma's old bridesmaid gowns or looking through her collection of dolls and toys from the 1920s. And her aunts had almost thirty more years of memories to sift through.

"I went through Mom's diaries last night. 1955 is missing," Aunt Ruth said.

Amy stopped and turned. Last year, when Robin had given all of Grandma Pearl's diaries to a graphic design student to digitize so everyone in the family could have their own copies, they'd discovered that several years were missing. "Maybe she hid it on purpose."

"Maybe." Tracy lifted a box from the top shelf. "Let's keep an eye out for that." She pointed to the old library table along one wall. "I started working on a way to organize everything. I put permanent markers, tape, zipper bags, and garbage bags on the table, and empty boxes underneath. The piles we've already sorted are marked." She gestured around the periphery where sheets of paper were tacked to the rough walls. The signs held labels like HISTORICAL SOCIETY, DONATE, SELL, DIVIDE, and MAKE COPIES.

"Quite the system." Once again, Aunt Abigail's usual upbeat tone seemed tamped down. It had to be hard to watch a lifetime of memories being triaged.

"Start wherever you want," Amy said. Aunt Abigail responded with a tight smile. This had once been her home. She'd grown up here. And now the house belonged to her oldest niece and her other nieces were sorting through things that had more meaning to her than to them. Amy felt her face warm. It wasn't her place to be giving her aunt permission.

Amy had wondered, over the years, why Aunt Abigail had never married. Mostly, she wished she knew if it had been a deliberate choice on her part, or if she'd never had the chance. A retired corporate executive, Aunt Abigail spent her time teaching Bible studies and speaking to women's groups. Amy imagined her life was full, yet the question of why she'd remained single still lingered. Had her heart been broken? Did she regret never having children? Though she was gregarious and flamboyant, Aunt Abigail was also a very private person, and Amy had a feeling her questions might never be answered.

Aunt Abigail lifted a box labeled DRESS PATTERNS from the middle shelf. "Violet was quite the seamstress, wasn't she?" She looked at Aunt Ruth. "I think she made a dress for you that I got to wear when you grew out of it."

Aunt Ruth nodded. "She made several matching dresses for you and me."

Old, brittle masking tape peeled off easily when Aunt Abigail pulled on one end. Dust rose and danced in the sunlight struggling through a dirt-streaked window. Aunt Abigail set the box on the floor in front of a folding chair and sat down to sort through the old patterns.

Robin and Aunt Ruth both grabbed boxes. Amy went to her "Picture Corner," and sat on a beanbag chair. She found the shoebox where she'd stashed black-and-white photographs from the 1950s that had once been mounted in a book with black pages and held in place by glue-backed photo corners, most of which had come loose. To her right were boxes with dividers labeled by decade. She took a handful of square pictures from the shoebox. Turning them face-down, she began reading the names and dates Grandma Pearl had written on the backs. After fifteen minutes of sorting, she found the name she'd been searching for. Violet. The caption read, *Ruthy and Abigail with Violet at Conway estate sale. June 11, 1955.* She stood as she turned it over. A young woman wearing polka-dot capri pants and a boat-necked shirt stood between two little girls with chin-length hair that curled around their faces. Hair that had probably been set in curls held in place with bobby pins. Amy walked across the attic. "Violet's last name was Conway, right?"

Aunt Ruth nodded. "Did you find something?"

Amy had intended to hand the photograph to Aunt Ruth but changed her mind and held it out to Aunt Abigail. "You two were adorable."

"We were, weren't we?" Aunt Abigail brought the picture closer to her face. "I vaguely remember this day. We helped her take things out of boxes and display them on tables, and she gave us each a new doll for helping." She looked at her sister. "Remember?"

"Yes. I'd wanted a Tiny Tears doll for what seemed like forever, and I couldn't believe it when she gave it to me." Aunt Ruth stepped over to Aunt Abigail and smiled at the picture, but after a moment, her smile faded. "That man. Something about him…" Amy stepped behind her as she pointed at a man standing several feet away and staring at Violet with what she could only describe as a sad smile.

"Violet knew him," Aunt Abigail said. "I'm not sure how I know that, but I'm sure of it."

"When did Violet and *River Dancer* disappear?" Robin asked.

Aunt Ruth shrugged. "Good question. I know there are some newspaper clippings somewhere, but…" She turned to Tracy. "There's probably an easier way to find out."

Tracy nodded. "I'll go get my laptop." She walked toward the stairs.

"Wait a sec." Amy held up one finger. When Tracy and Robin had come close enough to see the photo, she said, "That clock. Isn't that the one on the mantel in the guest room downstairs?"

Tracy squinted at the grandmother clock on a table filled with knickknacks. "It is. Which means…other things from the Conway estate could be here. Although I don't know how that would help us."

"Well"—Amy took a moment to think how to word the question—"if the Conway house sold, and Violet was living with our family, what did she do with things she wanted to keep?"

"I'm guessing she brought it all here," Aunt Abigail said, "intending to store it until she got married."

Amy felt a rush of adrenaline as a thought crystallized. "We all know it's highly unlikely that Grandma Pearl would have gotten rid of anything belonging to Violet. Unless she found out Violet was still alive and gave it to her, or found out she wasn't alive so there was no point in keeping it. Some of Violet's personal things could still be here. Letters or diaries that might tell us something. Or maybe we won't find anything, which also might tell us something."

Four pairs of eyes stared at her in bewilderment. "What?" Amy feigned surprise at their reactions. "Give it a minute and let the logic sink in. We hope we find something, but nothing could also be a better something than something."

After a moment of stunned silence, laughter bounced off the bare boards above them, Aunt Abigail's loudest of all. "Thank you, Amy dear, for making our search clear as mud. Now, ladies, let us continue our search for something or nothing or something in between."

Chapter Five

As Amy backed the car out of the driveway on Monday morning, her mind raced with all she needed to do at the end of the day. "Olivia is picking you up after school and taking you to the popcorn shop." Cheers rose behind her, but she cut them short. "The popcorn is for after supper, during the movie. I want you both to get your homework done before anything else. I have a meeting with Niesha at three forty-five that will take a couple of hours, and then I'm going to the office supply store in Quincy to pick up my business cards. I left a note about supper for Olivia. I told her to make two pizzas, one cheese, one sausage, so you'll both be happy."

"Pizza again?" The last word stretched out on a whine from Jana.

Pizza again? Did one of her children actually just use those two words together? What was that all about? They hadn't had pizza since…Friday. And two nights before that. Well, it was an easy meal. And she needed easy these days. "I promise I'll get back to real cooking as soon as I launch my Etsy store."

"You're going to miss the whole movie?" This from Matt.

Amy sighed and flipped on her turn signal. In truth, she was more than happy to miss this particular movie, even though she'd recommended it. *Pirate Dog* was the epitome of cheesiness, but her kids would love the tale of a wise-cracking dog named Scrappy, two lost little girls, and a ghost pirate ship. "If you love it, we'll watch it together—"

"When?"

She had to stop making promises she wouldn't keep. "Soon." Her voice sounded pathetically weak, even to herself. But she was doing this for them. It was the only way she could afford the family vacation she'd been dreaming about since she first decided to adopt Matt and Jana. They'd poured over brochures together, planning out their itinerary. Jana had drawn pictures of the clothes she wanted to buy for the trip. They'd even decided what kind of car they wanted to rent. She'd explained, more than once, that the trip would require some sacrifices from each of them.

It wasn't like she was this busy for selfish reasons. Plus, this was only for a season. They'd thank her for it when they got off the plane in Montana next summer. Like the woman in Proverbs 31, her children would rise up and call her blessed as they rode horses to a chuckwagon dinner at Golden Sky Dude Ranch.

In spite of the "It'll all be worth it" pep talk she'd given for the last two blocks, they were a somber trio walking into the school building. The biting wind didn't help. But it all made her twice as grateful than usual for the smiling face of her favorite niece. She stopped in front of Sara's open door and watched Jana slog down the hall to her second-grade classroom then slipped into Sara's room and perched on top of a student desk. Sara stopped watering the massive ficus tree that resided in her science corner, its leaves festooned with pictures of insects. "Tough morning?"

"Understatement."

"Talk." Sara leaned against her desk and folded her arms.

"I'm just having trouble…balancing."

Sara gave a sympathetic nod. "The proverbial too many plates in the air, or too much on your plate. One of those plate metaphors."

"Yes. But it's all important stuff. Launching my store, creating content, meeting with Niesha to work on the website." *And helping Carrie and Whitney and Brooke plan the fundraiser.* Seven months ago, she'd been in on the ground floor of opening a home for single moms and their children. Now that five women and nine children had moved in, they had a clear idea of what was needed, so the board had planned a housewarming shower and fundraiser for the week of Thanksgiving. But she didn't need to mention that obligation. It made her sound like one of those mothers who'd spread herself way too thin. That wasn't the case with her. This was just a season.

"And raising two kids. And rekindling a romance."

"True." Amy forced a smile. "I know. I need to cut something out. Or at least not take on anything more."

"I'll be praying you can take something off that full plate."

"Thank you."

Amy walked across the hall to her classroom. She inhaled deeply, as if she could take in the silence and hang on to it for the rest of the day. But the peace and quiet only lasted a few minutes. Outside her window, the first bus arrived. She glanced at her planner. Today was National Redhead Day. It wasn't a day she always called attention to, but it seemed appropriate this year. Aubrey Fritz, a girl in Sara's class with bright red corkscrew curls and freckles, who had just moved to Canton at the beginning of the year, was the brunt of some jokes that needed to stop. While she'd quickly made friends, several of the boys were merciless in their teasing and extremely creative in their nicknames. Today, Miss Allen would be reading *Sally Jean, the Bicycle Queen* and *Freckleface Strawberry*. It may not have started with a bang, but it would be a good day. Game face on, she stood at the door of her classroom and greeted each of her kids by name.

Charlotte Baker, the last one in line, gave a toothless grin as she walked in carrying a clear plastic container. "My mom and me baked Oreo-stuffed chocolate chip cookies. The recipe is in the bowl so you can see there aren't any nuts in it."

"Thank you." Amy took the container. "They look delicious." Why did her voice sound strained? She cleared her throat. "We'll have them after lunch." Amy closed the door, walked to her desk, and set the container down with a bit more force than needed, and then she chastised herself for her childish reaction. The prick of jealousy was ridiculous. She was not in competition with stay-at-home moms. Besides, she'd baked cookies with Jana just last week. Well, maybe not last week, but it hadn't been all that long ago.

She pasted on a smile she didn't feel. "Happy National Redhead Day! Today we're going to—"

"Ha! Frizzy Fritz has her own day!" Sebastian Diaz sparked a wave of laughter that ignited vicious glares from the girls who weren't joining in.

Amy sighed. Maybe it wasn't going to be such a great day after all.

The last student walked out, and Amy sank into her chair. The day had seemed twice as long as most. She'd been spoiled last year, her twenty-fourth year of teaching, but her first in the town where she'd grown up. Last year, she'd had a few talkative kids, but none who were outright rebellious. This year she had three boys and two girls who took great pleasure in getting under her skin and disrupting the schedule. The other seventeen were absolutely delightful, but it was hard to focus on the good when she didn't know when the next outburst would throw things off-kilter.

She picked up her phone and saw a missed call from Tracy five minutes earlier. She glanced at the clock. She didn't need to leave for a few minutes. She tapped on her sister's name then put the phone on speaker as she packed her canvas bag.

"Hey, Sis. I found something."

Tracy wrote a weekly newspaper column called Cantonbury Tales that highlighted local happenings and features about Canton residents and sites. She'd accessed the paper's archives from her laptop on Sunday, but hadn't come up with any information on the disappearance of *River Dancer*. Amy felt a surge of hope. "About Violet and the boat?"

"Yep. I spent my lunch break down in the basement looking at old microfiche film. In the June 22, 1955 issue, there's a picture of *River Dancer*. The subheading reads, 'Boat Missing from Private Slip.' I'll read it. 'Early last Friday morning, Canton resident Howard Allen reported that his 1940 Chris Craft cabin cruiser, pictured, was missing from its slip on the river just south of town. Anyone with any information should contact the Canton Police Department.'"

"That's it? No mention of Violet?"

"Not a word. I searched for her name, and all that came up was her father's obituary and a list of CSC students on the dean's list."

"That's strange." Amy stood and slid the strap of her bag over her shoulder. "The estate sale picture was taken on June 11. If that article came out on the twenty-second and said *River Dancer* went missing the previous Friday, that makes it, let's see...June 17, right? So the estate sale was only six days before *River Dancer* and Violet went missing. We should check records and see if the house sold at the auction. If it did, Violet might have just wanted to get away and start a new life somewhere else, far from all the memories of her dad."

"That's possible," Tracy said. "But that's something Grandma and Grandpa would have understood. They would have loaned her money if she needed it. And if the house sold, she would have had money for a bus or train or plane ticket. It doesn't make any sense that she'd feel the need to steal the boat."

"I agree. And maybe she didn't. Maybe the two things are completely separate. Just a bizarre coincidence."

"That would be beyond bizarre."

Once again, Amy had to agree. "There has to be more here. I think I'll make another visit to Silva and Katerina."

"Good idea."

Amy handed Niesha Carter the cappuccino that Lisa Frantz, Niesha's best friend, had made especially for her at Big O's Eats and Treats. "Lisa says hi and check your mail."

Niesha laughed. Amy knew the message was code, telling Niesha that Lisa had left her a clue in a mailbox that was part of an art display at Culver-Stockton College. The two women had been doing treasure hunts together since the first one they'd participated in with an art club at the college. "Come on in." Niesha gestured to an old wooden table she'd painted bright yellow that served as her desk. Two laptops were open side-by-side.

As Amy stepped over to the desk, she looked around the studio apartment that was far more "studio" than "apartment." Niesha had lived above the art gallery since graduating from CSC in May with a degree in art and an emphasis on graphic design. The exposed brick walls of her living room were covered in original oil and acrylic paintings and Niesha's stunning photography. Backlit shelves showcased her pottery creations, and many more were for sale in the gallery. Amy pointed at a large square canvas sporting Niesha's familiar logo—the letters *NC* with a black-outlined dragonfly. "That's new."

"I have a booth at the indoor flea market in St. Louis this winter. That will be part of my backdrop." Niesha smiled and winked. "Indiana's booth is right across from mine. He told me to tell you to come down and he'll give you a great deal on an old painting."

Amy couldn't help but laugh at that. The man they'd dubbed Indiana Jones manned the booth where they'd found Green Girl. After a bit of haggling, Robin had paid him for a stolen painting that was theirs all along.

One laptop screen displayed the logo Niesha had designed for Amy's "teacher2teachers" site and online store—two stylized hands, one holding a paper out to the other. "I can't tell you how much I love this." Amy took the chair to Niesha's left. "You did such a great job of captur—" Amy gasped and grabbed Niesha's hand. "What's this?" She gaped at a simple but elegant round diamond set in a wide gold band that adorned Niesha's ring finger.

Niesha beamed. "I wondered how long it would take you to see it. Emmett proposed on Sunday."

"Congratulations!" The young man she'd once thought had stolen Green Girl was, in fact, a growing Christian who had told the woman he loved that he wouldn't marry her until he had "a solid job and a decent nest egg." Amy gave her a one-armed hug. "How did he do it?"

"Oh, it was so sweet. He said he thought I should make matching mugs with our names on them, and when I sat down at my pottery wheel and started working the clay, the ring was embedded in it. I almost fell off my stool. Then he knelt on one knee and said... well, some really beautiful stuff." Her beautiful dark brown skin seemed to glow with happiness."

"I couldn't be happier for you two."

"Girl, you're next, right? How do you think Miles will propose? I can see him doing some grand gesture like hiring a skywriter or spelling it out in Christmas lights."

Amy laughed. "Well, first of all, I think that's a long way off, and, second, I have no idea. He's kind of a traditional guy, so maybe dinner at a fancy restaurant." She'd tried not to entertain too many thoughts about what a proposal could look like. Even though she felt closer to him every time they were together, it still wasn't a sure thing. She turned the focus back on Niesha. "Have you set a date?"

"Yes. Don't laugh."

"Why would I laugh?"

"Because we're getting married in two and a half weeks. Two days after Thanksgiving. Because"—she grinned—"drum roll, please... Emmett got accepted at the Metropolitan Police Academy in St. Louis. We found an apartment that needs some work, so we want to get it done before the semester starts."

Amy pressed her hands together. "That's wonderful. I hate to see you move away, but I'm so happy his dream is coming true. And you are the most organized person I know. You can pull it off."

"Well"—Niesha ducked her head then looked up with a sheepish expression—"I might be asking some friends for help."

"What kind of help?"

Niesha swiveled in her chair to face Amy. "Since we met, you have been so good to me. So nurturing and protective, and you're always there for me with encouragement and advice."

For a moment, Amy thought Niesha was going to burst into tears. As a child, the young woman had been bounced from foster home to foster home, so when Amy's family had embraced her like one of their own, she'd relished the sense of belonging. "You make all that easy." Amy meant that from the bottom of her heart.

"So does that mean you wouldn't mind, very much, um…giving me away?"

Chapter Six

Amy stood in front of the open refrigerator, gaping at the contents. Wednesday had always been pizza night. Matt and Jana had been invited to Kids Klub at a friend's church, and tonight would be a rush to finish homework, eat, and be out the door by six fifteen. Since her children were apparently in pizza overload, she had to think of something else. Not easy when she hadn't been shopping in over a week. She opened the freezer door. Corn dogs. Just as quick and easy, but not pizza. She pulled out the box and grabbed a frosty bag of peas. As she turned on the oven, her phone rang. Tracy. Amy answered, hoping her sister wasn't calling off their plans to dig around in Grandma's attic that evening.

"Hey, Sis. I found something. I couldn't wait until tonight. Did you know Aunt Abigail is staying for a few more days?"

"No, but I'm glad. I got the feeling she felt kind of left out of everything we're doing in the attic."

"I think you're right. Anyway, she and Aunt Ruth were talking about a picture they remembered of their whole family on *River Dancer*. They were both sure it was taken on Dad's fourth birthday. Their baby books are on the top shelf in the library, and I know Grandma put pictures of each of her kids' birthdays in those until they were six. Anyway, in with the baby books was Violet's bride book!"

"Really? Did you tell the aunts?"

"Not yet. I want to surprise them."

"I can't wait to see it. And speaking of weddings…" She told Tracy Niesha's news.

"That's exciting. Incredibly short notice. Tell me you didn't offer to help."

"Well, I suggested she look into the banquet room at River Dan's and talk to Whitney about a dress."

"That's all?"

"Um… Well… Okay, so I may have told her we'd throw her a bridal shower."

"We? You and Jana?"

"Funny. You know you love planning showers."

"Yes. Definitely. But not for a wedding that's in…seventeen days?"

"We'll keep it simple. I promise. We can have it at my house. I'll order cupcakes from Carrie's Cakes."

Tracy sighed. "Okay. I'll get all the paper products. Since Lisa's going to be her maid of honor, let's ask her to help. Maybe she can do games and keep track of gifts. Promise me you'll delegate. Your plate is already too full."

That phrase. Again. Amy closed her eyes, picturing a literal plate overflowing with too many good things. "You called about Violet's bride book." They were going to see each other in a couple of hours. She must have found something significant.

"Right. Great segue away from you overcommitting us. Anyway, tucked in the back of the book was a guest list. The bridal party is listed at the top. Silva and Katerina Pasternak were both in the wedding. I didn't recognize any other names other than the aunts and Dad. Then there were about a hundred guest names. But here's the interesting part. One name is scribbled out. I don't mean crossed out. A few had a line through them, like she knew they couldn't attend so why send an invitation, but on one, she'd actually torn the paper in the process of obliterating it. It's just completely blacked out."

"Interesting. I wonder if Katerina would know. I want to find out if they know the guy in the estate sale picture. I've left a couple of messages for them, but they haven't answered. Makes me think they're afraid of what I might ask them."

"Or maybe they're afraid of how they might have to answer."

Amy sat on a stool at the island in Tracy's kitchen, staring at the picture on the cover of the photo album under the words *Violet's Bride Book*. The man in the photo, who had to be Lenny, Violet's fiancé, wore dark pants and a pale green sport coat. Violet wore a white dress splashed with sunflowers and green leaves. A wide green belt circled her waist. The dress was accented with a string of white pearls. Looped over her arm was a purse the same shade of green as her belt. It had a metal closure and three sunflowers clustered on the front.

Lifting the cover, Amy found the sheet of loose-leaf notebook paper filled with handwritten names. She ran her finger across the line that had been so thoroughly inked out that the only thing visible was the dot of an *i* or *j* and the tail of a below-the-line letter. Not enough to go on.

Any adult who scribbled out a name with enough force to tear the paper had to have been angry. Did Violet do this? If so, what could have made her that mad?

The door opened, and her two aunts and cousin walked in. "Sorry we're late," Robin said. "I had a gabby customer at the end of the day." Robin owned Pearls of Wisdom, an antique shop in town. Her tales of the occasional irate or demanding customers were always entertaining.

"No worries," Tracy said. "I just finished the dishes. Let's head up to the attic before Amy's true love drops off her appendages."

Aunt Abigail looked shocked. Amy laughed and jumped in to explain. "That's what the curator of our local historical society calls my children."

Aunt Abigail raised one brow. "I hope she doesn't have any of her own."

"She doesn't. And it's just her brand of offbeat humor. Tawny Hagstrom is a wonderful person, once you get past the quirkiness."

"Sounds like this town is full of interesting characters. Including your 'true love.' Things getting serious with the handsome doctor?"

Amy pulled out her phone and read through her to-do list while making a show of ignoring her aunt. But she couldn't keep a tiny smile from lifting the corners of her lips, nor could she stop the warmth that filled her cheeks.

"They have a date night planned for Saturday," Tracy shared. "He's taking her to Carmine's Steak House in St. Louis."

Aunt Abigail whistled. "Then it is serious."

Amy rolled her eyes. As the matchmakers continued chatting about her love life, her phone rang. "Saved by the bell," she muttered.

Pasternaks flashed on her screen. Since they only had a landline, she didn't know which one she'd be talking to after she said hello.

"Is this Amy Allen?" Katerina shouted.

Amy smiled and whispered, "It's Katerina," to the other women. "I'll catch up with you." Into the phone she yelled, "This is Amy!" as she headed for the pantry where she could raise her voice without bothering anyone. Sadie, hoping for a treat, slipped in before she closed the door. She put her phone on speaker. "Thank you for calling me back!" She stretched her hand out, putting as much distance between her ears and the phone as possible. Should she tell Katerina to put in her hearing aids?

"Silva is a bit under the weather, so I don't think it would be a good idea for you to come here." Katerina sounded like she was reading the words off a teleprompter. "But we will call you when it's a good time."

"I'm sorry he's not feeling well." *If it's true.* "I'd like to show you a picture and see if you recognize the man in it. Do you have email?"

"Yes. It's p-a-s-t-e-r—" Silva's voice rumbled in the background, but Amy couldn't decipher the words. "I guess we changed it," Katerina shouted, her voice strained, but also with a tinge of what sounded like agitation. "I will call you when it's a good time. Goodbye."

Amy blinked at the black screen. "What was that all about?" she asked the dog.

Sadie gave a throaty whine. Amy laughed and reached for the jar of treats. She gave two commands, making the goldendoodle sit and shake before rewarding her with a bone-shaped biscuit. "Will you explain it to me if I give you this?"

Sadie merely grinned at her. When Amy opened the door, the dog ran to her rug in the corner of the kitchen and curled up.

"You're no help." Amy walked down the hall to the front foyer and up the stairway to the guest room. Laughter floated from the attic. When she reached the top of the attic stairs, she paused to thank God for the four women sitting in folding chairs around an old trunk. Who would she be without these nurturers who'd helped shape her life? Though she was an adult when her parents died, she was still in need of the support these four had provided by the bucketful.

"Learn anything?" Tracy asked her.

"Well, I learned that Katerina is a very…interesting person." She relayed the strange conversation.

"Funny she wasn't at least curious about the picture you wanted to show them," Robin said.

"I know. I'm sure she'd rehearsed what she wanted to say before she called. It was weird."

"Hmm." Aunt Ruth tilted her head. "Or maybe she'd rehearsed what Silva wanted her to say. I get the feeling he keeps a close rein on her."

Aunt Abigail nodded. "Definite possibility."

Amy gestured to a stack of papers and folders sitting on the trunk. "What did I miss?"

Tracy held out an envelope filled with white-bordered color snapshots, and Aunt Ruth showed her several typewritten pages stapled together. "This is the script for a women's club fashion show in 1955. Mom, Violet, Abigail, and I were all in it. I don't think it will help our search for clues, but it was held on"—Aunt Ruth flipped back to the front page—"June 4. Violet disappeared on June 17." She looked at Tracy. "You show the pictures, and I'll find the blurb to match."

Tracy held out a picture of a young woman wearing a navy blue suit with large safety pins attached in rows. Aunt Ruth scanned the copy and then began. "'Our next model could be a pinup girl. Doesn't she look sharp in her pinstriped suit?'"

Amy joined the others' laughter, and Tracy showed the next photo. A woman's head and arms stuck out of a large box decorated with windows, a door, and a chimney. "Bet I can guess this one," Amy said.

Aunt Ruth nodded. "'This young lady is feeling right at home in her cozy housecoat. The coat is well insulated for cold and vented for those hot summer days.'"

The next picture was of the aunts, ages seven and eight, holding hands. They wore fluffy white skirts with two big eyes and a puppy nose appliqued on each. A chubby young Aunt Abigail was turned to face her sister, making a fuzzy tail visible on her backside. Aunt Ruth read, "'Our youngest models can sit pretty and fetch admiring glances in their poodle skirts.'"

"That was so much fun," Aunt Abigail said.

"It was. But, against Mom's advice, I wore that skirt to school one day. It rained, and all of the cotton balls got soggy and fell off. I was mortified." Aunt Ruth laughed and then turned the page in her script as Tracy held out a picture of a woman in a bright red dress and matching jacket covered in paper flames. "'When winter comes,'" Aunt Ruth read, "'our next model will stay toasty warm in her new blazer.' Wait." She took the picture from Tracy. "That's Katerina."

Amy felt her eyes bug. The svelte redhead in the red dress was Katerina Pasternak?

"This must have been right after she and Silva got married," Aunt Ruth said.

The script for the next picture said, "'Here comes that card again.'" The photo showed a thirty-three-year-old Grandma Pearl wearing a sandwich board with a giant playing card painted on it. Amy sputtered. "We have to do this for the Pop's Place fundraiser." She wanted to call Carrie right then, when the ideas were fresh. Instead, she found her "PP Fundraiser" note on her phone and added the idea. When she tuned into the conversation again, Aunt Ruth was reading, "'Here we have the always fashionable yoke dress. Perfect for when you have company over…easy dress for fixing breakfast when you don't want to scramble for something to wear. Notice the lovely front and back yoke. Our model will always keep her sunny side up in this frock.'" The photo Tracy held out featured a woman in a bright yellow dress with a giant felt fried egg attached to the front. Amy assumed there was also one on the back of the dress.

Amy shook her head. "Perfectly corny. Where—"

"That's Violet," Aunt Ruth interrupted, peering closely at the photo. Suddenly, she gasped. "Her arm. I hadn't thought of that until just now. The dress was sleeveless, but she sewed sleeves on it the night before. I heard whispering after I was in bed, so I snuck into the hallway and hid behind Violet's door. Mom told her the dress was fine without sleeves, and suddenly Violet burst into tears. That's when I saw this purple bruise on her arm. She said she'd banged into a doorframe, but I could tell that wasn't the truth."

"Like someone had grabbed her?" Tracy asked.

"Exactly like that."

Amy stared at the picture, at the sleeve that covered a bruise. "I'm calling Katerina."

"She said they can't talk," Tracy reminded her.

Amy held her hand out to Aunt Abigail. "Can I use your phone? They won't recognize the number. There's a chance one of them will answer."

"But if they hear your voice…"

Tracy was right again.

Aunt Abigail took her phone out of her sweater pocket. "Show me the number. I'll call her."

They sat in breath-held silence as Aunt Abigail tapped in the number.

"Pasternak residence." Katerina's not-too-loud voice echoed through the speaker.

Aunt Abigail quickly explained who she was and asked if Katerina remembered anything about the bruises Violet got right before the style show.

After a moment of silence, Katerina said, "I…don't know…for sure, but…" Another pause. "I can't talk now. Goodbye."

June 3, 1955

Something is very wrong. Violet refuses to talk about it, but someone has hurt her. I found her tonight, altering her dress for the fashion show tomorrow. She has the most horrible-looking bruise on her arm. We got home from the style show rehearsal around eight thirty. She seemed agitated and said she wanted to take a walk before bed. Did she meet up with someone? Howard thinks my imagination has gone wild again. He believes Violet's story about hitting her arm on the door, but I simply cannot. What has she gotten herself into? Who would do such a thing, and why won't she tell me? I'm absolutely sure Lenny is not capable of causing her harm. He treasures her and treats her with such tenderness and respect.

I had been looking forward to a night of laughter tomorrow, but now all the joy has gone out of the fashion show for me. Still, we need to put on a good front for the girls and everyone attending. Tomorrow we'll spend the day making puff pastries that we'll stuff with chicken salad and cutting up fruit to be served in pineapples. We have little paper umbrellas to tape to the mint cups, and Maude is making her famous raspberry punch with an ice ring. It will all be lovely, but I know my mind will be elsewhere.

I need a plan. Lord, forgive me if I am doing something I should not, but I intend to start following Violet to see who she has contact with. Barbara from church is a dear friend and someone I can take into my confidence without fear she will spread gossip. She is a secretary at the college, and I know she will help me. Maura Childs, the daughter of one of the history professors, has joined the Women's Club. She's still in high school, but she does filing and research for her father after school, and she knows practically everyone on campus. I'm pretty sure she'd be willing to help keep an eye out for anyone harassing Violet.

Violet came to us in need of a family, and I intend to protect her and fight for her as if she were my own.

Chapter Seven

The second Saturday in November dawned bright and sunny. The wind that had buffeted the house for days had died down. Matt and Jana were still sleeping when Amy tiptoed out to the porch swing in her chenille bathrobe and fleece-lined slipper boots. This might well be the last day the weather would allow her to sit outside. She'd poured her coffee into a travel mug to keep it hot while she read her devotional and spent some time praying over the people and plans on her many lists. The most pressing thing being the meeting she was hosting in three hours for the Pop's Place fundraiser committee.

After the meeting, she'd have to rush to get to Matt's basketball tournament on time, and then she hoped to have at least an hour to spend in her office creating content for her Etsy store before getting ready for her date.

Why had she never before thought to monetize a thing she loved to do? Twenty-five years' worth of worksheets and handouts were crammed into files in her office and on her hard drive. Some needed to be updated, of course, but they were doing no one any good just gathering dust. She pictured a young teacher, fresh out of school, overjoyed to find Amy's user-friendly site filled with great printouts at a reasonable price.

The swing creaked as she settled onto it. With a push of one foot, she set it in motion. She breathed in the scent of fall. Someone in the neighborhood was up early burning leaves. Overhead, a flock of Canada geese honked as they headed south. She took a sip of coffee and then a bite of a cinnamon roll she'd found in the freezer, and she thanked God for the simple pleasures of a hot drink, a reheated delicacy, and a warm robe.

In her daily Bible reading, she'd reached the sixth chapter of the book of Matthew. She read a familiar passage out loud. "'Do not store up for yourselves treasures on earth, where moths and vermin destroy, and where thieves break in and steal. But store up for yourselves treasures in heaven, where moths and vermin do not destroy, and where thieves do not break in and steal. For where your treasure is, there your heart will be also.'"

Treasures in heaven. She'd just started a mental inventory, asking God to show her what she was clinging to, when her phone, deep in her robe pocket, vibrated.

Miles. Her heart did a little jump-skip as she thought about an entire kid-free evening with him. And then another thought. She scrunched her eyes shut and tried to remember if she'd asked Olivia to watch the four kids when they went to St. Louis. Yes. They were all set. Olivia, who now had her license and a car, which made Amy's life much easier, would arrive at four o'clock. Miles was showing up with his kids at quarter after. All was well. She smiled, breathed deep, and said, "Good morning."

"Good morning to you. I hear birds. Isn't it a bit nippy to be sitting on the porch in your bathrobe?"

In a sudden panic, Amy scanned the street and simultaneously smoothed her wild hair. She hadn't even taken the time to brush her teeth. "Where are you?"

"At home. Not stalking, I promise. I just know you."

"Yes, you do." And she was gradually coming to love that he did. She'd been so cautious about entering into anything more than friendship with the man whose heart she'd broken when she was eighteen. It had been her idea to move on. Even though Miles was headed off to college and on track for medical school, she'd been afraid that he wanted to return to Canton when he finished. And, like Scuffy the Tugboat in a book her grandmother had often read to her as a little girl, she thought she was "meant for bigger things." She did not miss God's sense of humor in bringing them both back to their hometown at the same time, thirty-plus years after their breakup.

"Would you like me to pick up Matt for the tournament, since you have your meeting?"

"That would be a huge help. Why don't you leave Natalie. That'll keep Jana from the awful fate of boredom."

"Sounds like a plan."

"So I get to see you three times today."

"Lucky girl. I think I'm going to fast all day so I have room for prime rib and mushroom risotto."

"Too late for me. I'm eating breakfast as we speak." Amy stared at her half-eaten cinnamon roll. When had she made them? A month ago, maybe? Jana had helped her. They'd had fun. When would she be able to carve out time for another mother-daughter baking day?

"I had my suit cleaned just for you."

"You own a suit?" she teased. "I thought you only wore scrubs and flannel shirts."

"I'll have you know I clean up real nice. And might I say, right back atcha, that I'm looking forward to seeing you in something other than schoolteacher clothes or jeans and T-shirts?"

"Youch. Point taken."

"I'm kidding. You always look amazing." Then, suddenly, he was singing.

Amy almost fell off the swing laughing as the words to Billy Joel's "Just the Way You Are" vibrated through the phone in the silky baritone she heard every Sunday as they stood together in church.

He stopped after a couple of lines, and her heart warmed as she laughed. "That was…something."

"Thank you. Thank you very much." His Elvis impression sent her into laughter again. It felt so good. Though she'd had several relationships since she was eighteen, no one had ever made her laugh like Miles Anderson.

"I should warn you that Matt is planning a photo shoot when you get here."

Miles laughed. "I heard a rumor about that. I think two little girls might have influenced him. This feels like some crazy prom date or something. Natalie has been giving me tips all week on what to talk about on a date. And don't act weird when I show up with flowers even though I've never brought them before. Apparently, it's mandatory when you put on a suit for a *real* date."

"I knew I loved that girl for a reason."

Silence met her lighthearted comment. "Miles?"

"I...love that you love my kids."

The emotion-roughened words brought tears to her eyes. Even though she'd entered into this renewed relationship promising herself she'd guard her heart by not getting too attached until she was sure where they were headed, what he'd said was true.

As they ended the call, she thought, not for the first time, that if anything ended this relationship, her heart would be fractured in three places. And the same would likely be true for him. And all four kids.

She couldn't let her mind go there. This was their second chance, and she wasn't going to do anything to mess it up. Shaking off the sudden intrusion of doubt, she tapped her phone to continue a search she'd started days ago—the search for Violet's obituary. Or Lenny's. She'd tried Violet Conway, Violet Therwood, Violet Conway-Therwood, and both Leonard and Lenny Therwood. Now she broadened it to *Violet + Canton*. Two people named Violet had died in Canton in the past seventy-five years. Two more were listed in the current census. There was a Violet Street in Canton, Ohio, and pictures of the Missouri violet in all its purple splendor. She tried several more combinations. And then...

> *Leonard J. Sherman, age 84, Rockport, IL, died Friday, October 30, 2019, at 2:30 a.m. at the Pike County Nursing Home in Rockport. He is survived by his wife, Violet C. Sherman, daughter Abby Ruth (Steven) Matson, and granddaughter Emily Matson.*

Leonard. Violet. *Abby Ruth.* Amy's breath caught for a moment before common sense returned. Leonard's last name was Therwood, not Sherman. She was grasping at straws. She locked her phone and brought her thoughts back to the here and now.

She had to go grocery shopping. Maybe this afternoon after the meeting. Amy moved bags and boxes around on the pantry shelf in search of something to make the kids for breakfast. They were out of eggs and milk, and only the crust ends of the last loaf of bread remained. As she scanned the top shelf, her gaze landed on a clear plastic bin labeled FALL. She'd brought it down from the attic at the end of September, thinking she'd get a jump on decorating. And there it sat, twelve days before Thanksgiving.

She looked away and spied a breakfast solution. Oatmeal. With the right toppings, the kids would never miss the milk.

Her phone dinged an incoming text. She pulled it out of her robe pocket and heaved a frustrated sigh when she saw that it was from an unknown number. Probably some scam. But then she caught three words. RIVER DAN SIGN. Leaning against the pantry shelves, she tapped on the text.

HI, MS. ALLEN. THIS IS JOSH JORDAN. MY DAD SAID YOU WANTED TO TALK TO ME ABOUT THE RIVER DAN SIGN. I'M OFF THIS WEEKEND AND DON'T HAVE PLANS. ANY CHANCE YOU'RE COMING INTO THE CITY? IF NOT, MAYBE WE CAN MEET HALFWAY. GIVE ME A CALL AND LET'S SEE IF WE CAN WORK SOMETHING OUT.

As a matter of fact, she was going to be in the city. On a date. Would Miles mind leaving a little early? She whipped off a text, asking him if they could leave at three instead of four, then grabbed the box of oatmeal and a few other things and turned, sucking in a breath when she bumped into Matt, standing in the pantry doorway. "Yikes. You scared me."

Matt gave a sleepy smile, and she hugged him with the arm that wasn't laden down with oatmeal, raisins, and brown sugar. He rubbed his eyes as he pulled away. "Where's my jersey?"

"It's in the… Oh, no."

"You forgot about the tournament."

"No! I'll be there. I just forgot about your jersey. I'll wash it out by hand real quick and stick it in the dryer."

"Okay." Matt's voice sounded flat. Several area youth groups were meeting at the high school for a basketball tournament. This was an important day. And his mother had forgotten an important detail. "I'm so sorry. I've had a lot on my—"

"You forgot about the movie too."

Amy let out a long, slow sigh. The kids had been talking about some movie—about a dog? A lovable monster?—for weeks. It would be out in a few days, and she'd promised to buy tickets for Friday. "We can still go. Maybe not on Friday, but…" Her voice evaporated as she watched him slog off to the stairs. This boy who'd faced so much uncertainty before coming to live with her was probably wondering right now if she'd meant all the promises she'd made when she adopted him. "Lord, help!" she whispered.

Moving at warp speed, she started the oatmeal, flew upstairs to grab the red jersey and matching shorts, checked to be sure there were socks and underwear in Matt's drawer, rushed back to the kitchen in time to catch the oatmeal as it was boiling over, cleared dirty dishes from the sink, put the clothes in sudsy water, yelled up the stairs for the kids to come down to eat, dished up oatmeal, and said a breathless prayer over the food as they started their meal.

After wringing out Matt's basketball clothes and sticking them in the dryer, it dawned on her that this might be the only time she'd have to connect with her "appendages" today. She filled a bowl for herself, indulged in a more-than-generous spoonful of sugar and a dollop of butter, and sat at the table.

She smiled at Matt, who stared into his bowl, pushing his oatmeal around with his spoon. "Pre-game jitters?" she asked.

Matt shrugged. "I guess."

"You'll do great. I know it would feel good to win, but this is mostly about having fun."

He didn't look up. "Uh huh."

"Can I use your video camera?"

That got his attention. Why did he look like she'd cornered him? "You don't have to do that. Pastor Gary is going to record it."

"Okay. Good. I suppose it's kind of embarrassing to have your mom screaming and yelling and videoing all at the same time." Especially when your mom was a teacher and most of the kids on the team knew who she was.

"Yeah." He went back to stirring the contents of his bowl, apparently with little interest in actually tasting it.

What the boy needed was a distraction, a change of subject. She pulled her phone out of her pocket. "I found a couple more things we can sign up for at Golden Sky. We can go rafting on the

Huckleberry River. It's nice and slow like a lazy river." She showed them a picture of a family in a bright yellow inflatable raft.

Jana smiled. "No waves?"

"No waves." She looked at Matt, but he was still staring at his bowl. "And how does archery sound?"

Jana's eyebrows rose. "With real bows and arrows?"

"Yep. They have them in all sizes." Again, she hoped for at least a glimmer of enthusiasm from her son. Nothing.

Her phone rang. She glanced at it, already determined not to answer it. *Pasternaks.* Why would either of them be calling? After the strange call from Katerina, she'd thought that was a closed door. If they were willing to talk in spite of whatever seemed to be frightening them, it was probably important. Her hand itched to snatch up the phone, but what if Matt interpreted that as another form of neglect?

Matt pushed his chair back. "I'm gonna go get ready."

He hadn't touched his oatmeal. "You didn't..." He was already loping up the stairs. With a sigh, Amy picked up the phone and answered with what she hoped sounded like cheerfulness.

"Amy. This is Katerina Pasternak. Can you hear me?" It was the same voice she'd heard on Wednesday, but at a much lower volume. Katerina must have remembered her hearing aids. But why was she whispering?

"I can hear you. Is everything all right?"

"I only have a minute. I think I know who hurt Violet, and I fear that if you get too close to the truth, you might get hurt too. Please don't—Gotta go."

Once again, Amy found herself staring at a black screen. She tapped out a quick text to Tracy, Robin, Aunt Ruth, and Aunt

Abigail, telling them what Katerina had said. THIS SOUNDS LIKE WHAT AUNT RUTH OVERHEARD V'S FIANCÉ SAY TO GRANDPA. THIS STARTED OUT FUN, BUT SHOULD WE CONTINUE? I WON'T BLAME ANY OF YOU IF YOU WANT TO STOP THIS SEARCH.

She waited, not sure what answers she was hoping for. She would not put her children at risk. But was it actually possible, after all these years, that there would be any real danger in trying to find out what happened in June of 1955?

Her phone dinged. Once, and then three more times in rapid succession.

Tracy: I'M STILL IN.

Robin: THIS JUST MAKES IT MORE INTERESTING!

Aunt Abigail: IF WE RUN INTO ANY REAL DANGER, WE'LL NEED TO STOP, BUT I'M ALL IN FOR NOW.

Aunt Ruth: YES, ABIGAIL AND I ARE TEXTING FROM DIFFERENT ROOMS IN THE SAME HOUSE LIKE TEENAGERS. ANYONE INVOLVED BACK THEN WOULD LIKELY BE IN THEIR NINETIES OR OLDER, IF THEY'RE STILL ALIVE. I'M IN!

Chapter Eight

Amy took a deep breath and plopped into a kitchen chair. She looked around the table and gave a wan smile to Tracy, Whitney Alloca, Carrie Ellis, and Brooke Shepherd. "Can we pray before we start?"

"I'll pray," Carrie offered. "Looks like you need a moment to just close your eyes." Her words exuded sympathy. As the mom of a seven-year-old whose brain and body always operated at full speed, Carrie understood. She bowed her head. "Lord, thank You for the privilege of helping young moms and their children. We are honored to be called to serve You in this way, but we know You've called us first to our own families, so help us to use our time wisely and to know when to say no. Please bless Pop's Place and everyone who is living there now and will in the future. Grant us wisdom as we work out the details for this fundraiser. We pray in the name of Jesus. Amen."

Know when to say no. If Amy didn't know that Carrie was also a stretched-thin mom, she'd wonder if Tracy had been talking to her about her concerns for Amy's busyness. Reassured that Carrie wasn't pointing fingers at her, she started the meeting by going over the budget, happy to get the necessary but not fun part out of the way first.

"Before I bring up the next thing, I want to echo what Carrie prayed about saying no. I want you all to feel free to tell me this is a crazy idea and we don't have enough time to prepare." With that, she laid out the photos and script from the 1955 fashion show.

Whitney was the first to react. "This is awesome!" Today Whitney's short hair was a strangely beautiful mix of chestnut brown and wide streaks of burnt orange. Since all of the fall-colored clothes were on sale this week at Pop Rocks Vintage, she was a walking advertisement in an oversized moss-green turtleneck over dark tan faux suede pants. When she'd walked in, the first words out of her mouth had been, "I know, I know, I look like a tree." She picked up a picture with each hand. "I've got the perfect red dress for this and a navy suit that will work for the pinstripes. We *have* to do this."

Carrie nodded. "I agree. It's perfect. We've got the moms' testimonies, and then Rose Napolitano and Columbia Burke are speaking, then a solo. That's all going to be encouraging but kind of somber. We need some fun." Her lips parted, and one finger shot in the air. "I'll decorate the cupcakes to coordinate with the fashion show." She tapped a nail on one picture then another. "This will be so fun. I can do fondant fried eggs, and flames and Red Hots on some, and I've bought diaper pins made out of sugar for baby showers before." She rubbed the palms of her hands together. "I can't wait to start sketching ideas."

Amy grinned at Carrie's excitement. She'd witnessed her creative genius at work before. A brainstorming session for Carrie's Cakes was always fun. After Tracy offered to be the photographer for the show, Amy turned to the only person who hadn't yet chimed in. "Brooke?"

"Definitely." Her eyes lit when she smiled. Brooke's attitude and even her appearance had changed drastically since moving into Pop's Place six months earlier. Before that, she and her son, Gavin, had been living in a storage shed, essentially homeless. Amy marveled at the way God had provided a beautiful old Victorian house that Brooke, Gavin, and several other families now called home. "One question. Can the Pop's Place Princesses be in it?"

The women smiled at the name one of the residents had coined, and all three nodded. "That would be amazing," Amy said. "If we scramble"—she pointed at the picture of the yoke dress and winked—"we can pull this off. We've got eleven days, ladies."

Eleven days. And fourteen until Niesha's wedding. She had a bridal shower to plan.

Know when to say no. The words floated through her mind like the banner at the bottom of the nightly news. Only this time it didn't sound like Carrie's voice. Or her own. Was God trying to tell her something? *Okay. From now on, I'm not taking on anything new.*

"...if we could paint the living room at Pop's Place before we start decorating for Christmas." Brooke's voice broke through the running to-do chant in Amy's brain. "We don't mind doing the work, but..."

"It would be a lot easier if the kids weren't there, right?" Carrie said.

Brooke's smile was part grimace. "I hate to ask."

"No prob," Whitney said. "That's what we're here for."

Amy wrestled for a moment, knowing that, of all the women present, she had the largest kid-friendly space in her home. But the heavenly nudge was still fresh.

"I have an idea," Carrie said. "How about we have a Popelstopp popcorn and movie party at Faith Church for all the Pop's Place kids some night after Thanksgiving?"

"That sounds fun," Amy said. Much to her own surprise, and maybe to the others at the table, she didn't offer to help. It was one small victory against overcommitment, but it was a start.

Amy fumbled her lipstick tube, and it fell into the sink. Picking it up, she looked frantically at the clock face reflected in the bathroom mirror. The second hand seemed to be moving faster than usual. She had ten minutes to finish primping. "I can do this. I can do this." She slowed her breathing with the chant.

"Do what?" Jana stood in the doorway.

"Get ready on time." Her voice was distorted as she applied Toasted Almond color to her lips.

"You look pretty."

"Thank you, honey."

"Can Natalie and I make cookies with Olivia tonight?"

Amy's swallow was audible. Earlier, after the final tournament game ended—the games she'd arrived at only five minutes late—she'd run to the store and picked up some quick-fix, mostly healthy, meals and cookie ingredients. She'd planned to bake with Jana tomorrow. Or soon, anyway. She managed a smile. "That would be fun."

"Yes!" Jana turned to leave.

Amy stopped her. "Could you girls do me a big favor? I got out some craft things, and there's a box of candles and pumpkins and flowers on the top shelf in the pantry. Do you want—"

"We can decorate for Thanksgiving? Seriously? Yes! This is going to be so, so fun." Jana wrapped her arms around Amy's middle then ran out of the room, leaving Amy alone to stare at her reflection. Small victories. She should be the one baking and decorating with her daughter, but at least she'd planned some fun. And they'd have a decent supper.

She'd set her hair in hot rollers and, even in her hurry, had taken more time on makeup than she did during the week. The shimmery black dress camouflaged the places she'd never had to think about back when she worked out four times a week. But, she thought for the hundredth time, she'd never trade the crazy, busy life she lived now for her old life that included time at the gym.

Though she would like a little less crazy and busy.

The doorbell rang. She grabbed her black clutch, slipped into classic black patent leather heels, and ran down the stairs.

The sight at the bottom took her breath away. Miles wore a charcoal-gray suit with a white shirt and black tie with silver stripes. In his hand was a bouquet of bright orange and yellow flowers. But it was the look in his eyes that made her forget how to draw another breath.

"You look amazing." He held out the bouquet.

She gasped. "You…brought me flowers? Wow. I can't believe it. I love, love, love flowers, but I didn't expect them. They're beautiful. This is so wonderful." As Matt snapped pictures, she played up the shock exactly like Miles had told her not to, reveling in his eye roll.

Natalie's skinny elbow shot out, jabbing her dad just above the waist. "I told you," she whispered.

Two little girls gazed with eyes of wonder as Miles helped her with her coat, pulling her hair gently out from under the collar. After a few last-minute instructions to Olivia, they hugged all four kids. She was relieved when Matt responded with his usual warmth. Getting to his game almost on time had seemed to heal the tension between them.

As they walked to Miles's Jeep, he rested his hand on her back. "Is everything okay with Matt?"

Amy felt a twinge of disappointment. She'd hoped this would be a night to just focus on the two of them. "He's been a little frustrated with his mother lately." She hoped her honesty wouldn't launch them into a discussion about her busyness. "I forgot to wash his jersey."

"I think it might be more than that. Colton said he's been really quiet the last couple of days. He thinks one of the seventh-grade boys might be picking on him."

Amy's heart sank. Though it hadn't been seamless, the kids had made a good transition into a new school last year, both of them making friends quickly. "Matt hasn't said anything. Who is it?"

"I don't know. I'll talk to Colton some more tomorrow. But for now, let's just enjoy the evening." Her reached for the door handle, leaning close to her ear. "I've been looking forward to this all week."

"Me too." And she meant it. But the man's timing was horrible. Why had he brought up concerns about her son right now? *Lord, clear my mind and give me peace. Grant me wisdom with Matt and help him with whatever he's dealing with, but for now, let me focus on Miles.*

She could do this. Tonight she would leave all other cares behind and focus only on the man who smiled at her with that incredible smile as he closed her door. Tonight was all about the two of them.

Well, it would be after they talked to Josh Jordan and hopefully added a few puzzle pieces to the mystery of Violet Conway and *River Dancer*.

Josh Jordan was in his midtwenties and at least six foot two. His third-story loft had high ceilings, old wood floors, exposed brick, and a view of the St. Louis arch. As Josh fixed coffee, Amy exclaimed over his surprisingly artsy décor. Several massive unframed paintings of historic landmarks in the city hung behind a white leather sectional. "I have to say, this is not what I pictured for a bachelor firefighter's apartment."

Josh laughed and handed them each a heavy black mug. "My fiancée owns an art gallery."

"That explains it," Miles said. "After I got out of med school, I decorated my first place by cruising the upscale neighborhoods the night before the once-a-month trash pickup of big items. Early Poverty style."

With a nod that seemed to say, "I get that," Josh gestured toward the sectional. "My college dorm room looked like our bunk room at the station. Nothing on the walls, no rugs, purely functional.

I slept in a sleeping bag on a bare mattress. The first time my then-girlfriend saw it, she was horrified. I think it might have been the part about only washing the sleeping bag every few months that got to her. I thought she was going to dump me right then and there, but, as you can see, she has reformed me."

When they'd all settled on the span of white leather, Josh said, "Why don't you tell me about the boat, and then I'll fill you in on everything we found."

Everything? Amy almost jumped out of her cushy seat, but she managed to get her too-rapid breathing under control and told him about the disappearance of *River Dancer*. When she got to the part about Violet, his eyes widened.

"Whoa. Wow. Um, let me start at the beginning." Josh moved to the edge of the couch. "Two years ago last May, a couple of buddies and I planned a kayaking trip from here, Quincy Bay, down to John Hay. All was smooth until the last day, about a mile before we were going to get off the river. I was taking a video, so I'd rested my paddle, and all of a sudden the current forced my kayak toward a small outcropping. Before I could grab my paddle and steer, I rammed into a tangle of exposed roots and tipped. This is the part I didn't tell my dad," he said in a conspiratorial whisper. "I got pulled under, and my shirt got stuck on a bunch of undergrowth. I've taken underwater rescue classes, but I was on the verge of blacking out when I was finally able to rip my shirt and get free. Somehow, I managed to get up on top of my kayak. When my buddies maneuvered back to me, I wasn't breathing. It took them a few minutes to revive me."

Amy gasped, which made Josh smile. "You know I risk my life for a living, right?"

She shook her head and glanced at Miles. "Remind me to tell our boys to never become firefighters."

Miles laughed. "It's every boy's dream." He looked at Josh. "Go on."

"When they got me up on the bank, I remembered a vision I'd had while I was unconscious. I was about to give up, when I saw my dad's name, 'Dan,' right in front of my face. I was sure God was telling me to keep fighting. Right after that, I pulled as hard as I could and broke free. My foot found something flat, and I was able to push against it to clear the surface. I realized later that was the board with 'River Dan' on it."

Amy rubbed her sleeves, trying to calm the bumps his story had raised. "That's more amazing than you know. My aunt told me that every time my grandparents took anyone out in the boat, my grandmother would pray, asking God to bless and protect every person who set foot on *River Dancer*."

It was Josh's turn to rub his arms. "Wow. That just confirms the feeling I had that I was destined to find the things that were buried under that tree."

Chapter Nine

Things? Buried? Did Josh use the word in the sense of being hidden? Or did he actually think the board, and whatever else he'd found, had been placed there deliberately? Amy opened her mouth to barrage him with questions, but Miles spoke before she had a chance.

"So you figured out it wasn't a vision...," he prompted.

"Yeah. When my head cleared, I remembered details, like the green lichen growing all over it. There was green under my fingernails, so I knew I'd actually touched it. My buddies didn't want me to, but I went back in. Something about it seemed...I don't know. Critical. Like it was there just waiting for me to find it."

"How far down was it?" Miles asked.

"Ten to twelve feet, I'd guess. One of the guys had a waterproof flashlight. The tree had actually grown around the board, almost like it had become part of the root system. It took four of us, taking turns, about an hour to wiggle it free."

"Your dad made it sound like it was right on the surface, an easy find." Amy's brain stuttered. It was too easy to picture Matt in a few short years, getting himself into risky situations she'd never hear about.

"Yeah, well..." Josh grinned. "My parents were paying for half my education. I didn't want to give them any reason to doubt my ability to take care of myself and make wise decisions."

Amy shook her head. "You said you'd tell us about everything you found. There was more?"

"Yes." Josh rubbed his palms on his knees and stood. "I wasn't sure the two things were connected." He talked as he walked to a white-painted antique armoire and opened it. "Don't tell my fiancée I kept this. She threw it away, but I fished it from the trash and spread it out in my storage room in the basement to dry out. Life got crazy, and I forgot about it until my dad told me about meeting you."

What was "it"? Amy slid to the edge of the white sofa and tried not to look like a child on Christmas morning, but the suspense was unbearable. When Josh finally turned around, he held a gray grocery bag in his hands. "This was stuffed between tree roots under the board." He didn't pull the item out until he came back around the corner of the sectional. Then he removed something brown and cracked and about the size of a nine-by-twelve envelope. She couldn't tell what it was until he set it on the coffee table.

Amy gasped. In front of her was an old, shriveled leather purse with a metal clasp and looped handles. In spots, a bit of faded, dirty green showed through the brown. And on the front she saw three round, raised circles with nubs that had once clearly been petals. "Sunflower petals. It's Violet's purse."

"You're sure?" Miles asked.

"Yes. I saw it in a photograph." She looked at Josh. "What was in it?"

He motioned for her to open it. "There was a soggy mass of what I'm guessing was paper at the bottom. There were no words left on anything."

Amy set the grocery bag on her lap to protect her dress then picked up the purse. The metal clasp that consisted of two tiny balls on curved posts that intertwined was now all reddish-brown with rust. She twisted it, sending flecks of rust falling onto the bag. Inside, a web of threads that must have once been a satin lining obstructed her view of the contents. Cautiously, she slid her hand in and pulled out the first thing she touched. Cylindrical. A tarnished lipstick tube.

"Open it," Josh said.

Careful to pull the top up perfectly straight, she removed it. A quarter inch of red lip color was still there, intact. She wished her aunts were here. Had they played dress-up with this very lipstick?

At the bottom of the purse she found a pen, a rusted nail file, a checkbook cover, and a brown-crusted wallet that looked like it was once blue. Inside a flap in the wallet fastened with a snap she found three quarters, too tarnished to read the date, and what she guessed were several bus tokens. If Violet had kept pictures in the plastic sleeves made for that purpose, or had carried a driver's license or any other kind of identification, they had all disintegrated. Amy opened the pocket meant to hold paper money and was startled to find a five-dollar bill, still recognizable. And then her fingers wrapped around a small, flat object on the bottom of the purse. She held it up. A skeleton key.

"Isn't that strange for 1955?" Miles asked. "Are there any doors in Jeff and Tracy's house that still use them?"

"Not now, but who knows about sixty-plus years ago."

"It's all yours," Josh said. "I'm getting married in two months, and it has to be gone by then." He smiled. "I'd appreciate it if you'd let me know what you find out."

"Of course." Amy put everything carefully back in the purse and wrapped it up in the bag. As she reached for her own purse, she remembered what she'd wanted to ask him. "You used the word 'buried.'" She hadn't actually posed a question, yet she waited for his answer.

"Yes. At first I thought they were just random things, caught in the current like my kayak. Then I wondered if the board could have been part of a boat, and that made me think it might have wrecked right there. But the edge that's clean cut seemed odd. Anyway, now that you've told me about the boat and the girl going missing at the same time, I have a theory. But I don't want to creep you out."

"Tell us," Miles said.

"Well, I went back a few weeks after we found this and studied the riverbank. There's evidence that a lot of erosion has occurred there over the years. The oak tree was huge, maybe a hundred years old. I'm no scientist, but I'd guess when it started growing, it wasn't in the water. I think it's likely it was maybe a few feet, or even a couple of yards, from the edge of the river."

Amy took a moment to process. "So…" She didn't want to think of the implications of what she was about to say. "You're saying you think the board and the purse could have been…"

"Buried there. In the ground. Intentionally."

"This is the best risotto I've ever tasted." Amy savored another bite of the creamy rice with mushrooms as she looked around the dining room at Carmine's.

"I agree." His voice sounded distracted.

"Something wrong?"

A small divot formed in his right cheek as he smiled sheepishly. "I need to apologize for bringing up the thing about Matt. That was dumb. It's probably nothing, and now I'm sure it's been playing in the back of your mind all evening."

"I can't say I've forgotten about it, but I prayed and reminded myself that I can't do anything about it now. On Monday I'll talk to Kelly and try to find out what's going on."

His eyes darkened. "Are you sure talking to the principal is the best place to start? If the kid who's been picking on him finds out Matt's mom is fighting his battles for him, things could get worse."

"Are you speaking from firsthand experience?"

Miles tilted his head. "You're a very perceptive woman. You were also the cause of my firsthand experience."

"What? When?"

"Before we started dating. Right before. Did you know Tommy Cooper had a crush on you?"

Amy wrinkled her nose. She barely remembered the boy. He was big, a football player. She couldn't remember a single conversation she'd had with him. "I did not."

"Well, he did. And when someone told him I asked you out, he decided to make my life miserable. After he gave me a shiner, my dad talked to Principal Adams. After that, Tommy and three guys from the football team met me outside of school."

"I remember you had a black eye. You said"—her thoughts went immediately to Violet—"you ran into a post. What else did he do, they do, to you?"

He smiled. "They were big, and strong, but they weren't fast. I outran them. And I may have told a few guys on the team. That was the end of that."

"So maybe Matt needs a better strategy than his mom fighting his battles."

"Maybe. Talk to him, and let's pray on it. For now, let's enjoy our dinner."

Amy had been determined not to talk about Violet's purse or what they'd found in it or the fact that Josh finding it under the board from *River Dancer*'s stern seemed to prove that Violet had been on the boat when it...what? Now she had another thing to not talk about.

To extricate her thoughts from dark places, she stared up at the orange and yellow blown-glass light fixture right over Miles's head. The curlicued tentacles on the sun-like orb looked like the work of Dale Chihuly, the artist who broke traditional glassblowing rules of symmetry by using physics to encourage molten glass to "find its own shape." She'd seen his work at an exhibition in Boston years ago when she went there for a teachers' convention.

"...haven't gotten it right yet."

Amy blinked at Miles. "I'm...sorry. What did you say?" She was failing at being present in the moment.

"I said I've tried making mushroom risotto, but it's never as good as this." He tilted his head again. "Your head is in the purse, isn't it?"

She laughed. "I've been accused of having my head in the clouds before, but no one has ever accused me of having my head in a purse."

His smile seemed a bit tight. "Tell me your theory of how it got there."

"How my head got in the purse?" This brought a genuine smile. "Actually, I was thinking about the light fixture." She pointed up. "What does it remind you of? First thing that comes to mind."

"Medusa."

"Ew." Picturing the mythological creature whose head sprouted live snakes instead of hair, she lifted a forkful of the deep-fried onion strings that garnished her rack of lamb. "I don't think I can finish these now."

"She's not real, you know." His deadpan expression made her laugh all over again. "So what does the light remind you of?"

Amy stared at the light fixture again. This time she saw streaks of bright green mingled with the orange and yellow. The colors of sunflowers. Like the ones she'd seen in the picture of Violet and Lenny. "It reminds me of a sunflower." Miles wouldn't make the connection. Men weren't into details, especially the details of a—

"Like on the purse."

She grimaced and then quickly tried to hide it by taking a sip of her water. After she swallowed, she looked into his eyes. "Just like a sunflower." She lifted another forkful of risotto, but instead of raising it to her mouth, she simply stared at it. "Porcini mushrooms."

"Huh?"

"You wanted to know the secret ingredient. I think they use dried porcini mushrooms. They have a richer flavor than fresh oyster or shitake mushrooms, and I think that's where the little bit of chewiness comes from. And they're rich in other ways too. Like sixty dollars a pound rich."

Miles's eyes seemed to twinkle. "You are a wonder."

"Is that a good thing? Do I keep you wondering?"

He smiled. "Sometimes. Like now, when you're keeping a running conversation about chandeliers and mushrooms when I know you really want to talk about a missing boat and a buried purse."

"Miles." She let out an exasperated sigh. "Tonight, I just want to enjoy being with you in this amazing place."

"Uh-huh." His tone was straight-up patronizing.

The guy had X-ray vision. She'd read many novels depicting a heroine who longed for a man who could read her mind. The man who sat across from her possessed that skill, at least at times, but it completely unnerved her. She studied his smile, trying to turn his weapon against him. What she saw in that smirky smile was not a man annoyed with her because she was distracted. What she saw, or thought she did, anyway, was something very different. It was her turn to smirk. "*You* want to talk about the mystery."

"Well, yeah. Maybe." His sheepish smile was adorable. "I mean, we're still enjoying time together, and we need *something* to talk about."

Amy's laugh bounced off the snaky sunflower light fixture. "Yes, we do. So tell me your thoughts from what we learned."

"I'm stuck on the word 'buried.' Do you think it's possible..."

He didn't have to finish the question. She knew exactly where this thought trail was heading. "I keep trying not to think what I'm pretty sure you're thinking."

"Let's let the eight-hundred-pound gorilla out of its cage." He took a deep breath. "If it was deliberately buried, why? And then, that brings up another question. Is it possible there's something else buried there?"

"Or some*one* else?"

June 4, 1955

The fashion show was a huge success. I'm sure some of the older women haven't laughed that hard in decades. My girls were so, so adorable in their "poodle" skirts. Shirley Boyd took pictures of everyone, and I can't wait to see them. Everything went off without a hitch, except for Maude's aspic salad. I'm laughing now, just thinking about it, but I did feel sorry for her at the time. It was beautiful, with finely chopped celery, carrots, and cauliflower layered in clear gelatin. She'd used a ring mold and had decorated it with dollops of mayonnaise and tiny tomatoes. It looked more like a wedding cake than a salad. Sadly, though I'm laughing hysterically now, the stifling summer heat in the church basement was just too much for it. We'd needed all the room in the refrigerator for the chicken salad puffs, so someone, thankfully not me, took the aspic out and set it on the buffet table before we started the fashion show. By the time we finished, poor Maude's creation was nothing but an eroded mound of quivering jelly surrounded by a mote of floating vegetables! To her credit, she recovered quickly and said she'd take it home and make soup out of it.

Violet seemed in a much better mood for most of the night. Of course, I watched her like a hawk. She laughed with

Katerina as they came down the steps before we ate, then suddenly she froze and almost tripped. I tried to figure out what, or who, she'd seen. It appeared she was looking at a table where three members of the Culver-Stockton auxiliary sat. Minerva Sanders, Corrine Williams, and Sally Janvier. Sally was at the church last night, helping with rehearsal, so I'm quite sure it wasn't her. Possibly Corrine, who was Vi's father's secretary for years. I have no idea what spooked her. Lord, I need wisdom!

Chapter Ten

"Everybody wash your hands before we eat," Tracy called into the library.

The entire family had gathered for Sunday dinner. Matt and Jana were playing a guessing game in the living room with the little ones, Corbin, Emerson, Aiden, and Zoe. Jeff and Tracy's daughter-in-law, Anna, dozed by the fireplace after nursing baby number three, Elizabeth Pearl, and the rest of the adults and Kai, the in-between one, sat at the table in the library, inspecting the contents of Violet's purse. Dutifully, they all scrubbed their hands for dinner while Tracy rolled up the newspaper she'd insisted they lay down before setting the purse on the table, because "Who knows what little critters could still be living in it."

Today's dinner theme, setting the mood for the topic of the day, was favorite dishes from the aunts' childhood. Earlier in the week, Amy had suggested family style "like the old days" instead of the usual Sunday buffet on the kitchen island. The idea had been met with matching eye rolls from her aunts, who didn't think of the fifties as ancient history. After a bit of feigned indignation, they'd started a barrage of texts sharing recipes.

After Aunt Abigail prayed over their meal, the children sat at the disinfected library table, the grownups and little ones found places in the dining room as usual, and they began passing dishes and platters filled with tuna noodle casserole topped with potato chips, three bean salad, meat loaf, mashed potatoes, Parker House rolls, and lime Jell-O with pineapple and cottage cheese in it. Dessert would be two varieties of icebox cake.

"The skeleton key is the most intriguing," Tracy said, continuing the discussion that had begun earlier. "I can't imagine that any houses, this one included, would have had front door locks like that in the 1950s. I suppose it could have been for an inside room. It makes sense that Violet would have wanted to lock her bedroom when there were nosy little girls in the house." She winked at the aunts.

Aunt Ruth laughed. "We did sneak into her room on occasion. Her wedding gown hung on the back of the door in a clear plastic bag. Every chance I got, I'd go in and just stare at it. It was gorgeous."

Amy ladled gravy onto her mashed potatoes. "Where do we go from here?"

"I'd like to search the place where the guy found the purse." Jeff broke a roll and buttered it while glancing around the table, waiting for someone to respond.

"The water is ten to twelve feet deep," Amy said. "And it's November."

"And your point is?" Challenge sparked in his eyes.

"And the current was strong enough to tip the guy's kayak," Tracy added.

"You too?" Jeff grinned at his wife. "Here I am, trying to help, and this is what I get?"

Chad raised his hand. "I'm in. Name the time and place, Dad, and I'll bring scuba gear. I mean, I'll dig my scuba gear out of your garage and bring it." When he caught Anna glaring at him, he added, "If it's okay with my wife, of course." He put his arm around her and stroked the baby's head. "You know I'd never, ever, do anything without your enthusiastic support, sweetheart."

"Did I raise that boy right, or what?" Jeff said.

"I'm in if my wife lets me." Kevin put his arm around Sara and looked at his father-in-law with a silly half smile, as if begging for approval.

"You're a good man, Kevin Willey. My daughter is a blessed woman."

Tracy made a gagging sound. "Mind if I cut into this love fest, boys? You're all brilliant and wonderful, but this could be dangerous, couldn't it?" She held up a finger. "Truth. And nothing but the truth."

"In truth," Jeff said, drawing out the word, "if there are three of us, I think we'll be fine."

"A buddy of mine has a pontoon boat," Terry said. "I'm sure he'd let us borrow it if you don't mind me tagging along. Saturday?"

"That would be a huge help," Jeff said. He smiled at Tracy. "What could go wrong with four of us? Saturday is supposed to be in the sixties and sunny, but we'll keep an eye on it and check the river depth and—"

"If Dad's going, I'm going."

They all turned to see Kai leaning against the arched doorway leading to the library. Matt stood right beside him. "Me too."

Grateful to see her son looking more carefree than he had the day before, Amy wanted to make that happen. Miles and the kids had a standing invite for Sunday dinner, but he'd promised an elderly neighbor he'd put up her Christmas lights before the weather got too cold. Amy knew what he'd say if he were here. "I'm sure

Miles would love to be part of this too. We can probably use his boat. And by 'we,' I'm assuming women and children are included."

Jeff winked at Tracy. "Pretty sure the men don't have veto power on that."

"Yes!" Matt pumped the air and then high-fived Kai. "We're going on a treasure hunt!"

After the dishes were done, the men and older boys went out to the garage to examine the scuba gear Jeff and Chad hadn't used since a trip to Mexico before Corbin was born. Anna and Sara settled the little ones in front of an episode of *Daniel Tiger* in hopes that they'd all fall asleep, and the women and Jana gathered at the Eastlake table that had witnessed four generations of family gatherings.

Amy's phone rang. Niesha. They exchanged greetings, and then Niesha asked if Amy was home. "I'm at my sister's, probably for a couple more hours," Amy told her.

"I printed out several nine-by-twelve envelopes with your return address and new logo. I don't think a picture would do them justice. Can I drop them off at Tracy's?"

"Of course. There might be a piece of cake waiting for you when you get here."

Amy hung up then held out the key she'd found in Violet's purse. She'd seen a blue and white metal bottle of brass cleaner in Tracy's pantry—the same bottle she remembered using as a young teen to clean a decorative brass plate missionaries to India had given their grandparents—and had teased her sister that she was becoming a pack rat like Katerina. After using the eye-watering solution on the key, it gleamed when she held it up to the overhead light. "This is too small to be a door key." She handed it to Robin, their resident antiques expert.

"I agree. It's too large to fit a jewelry box or dresser drawer, but it does seem too small for a door. A steamer trunk, maybe?"

Tracy set a pot of cinnamon apple tea on the table. "There are a couple of those in the attic."

As they passed the teapot, filling cups Grandma Pearl had used to serve tea to friends back in the fifties and before, Jana paged through Violet's bride book. Aunt Ruth set a jar of wildflower honey on the table then halted midstep. "That's it. That's Violet's dress." A Vogue dress pattern was stapled to a page in the book. On it was one of the most sophisticated vintage dress designs Amy had ever seen. Aunt Ruth leaned down and read the description pasted under the pattern.

"'This romantic design features a sheer floral lace bodice and back, a scalloped Sabrina-style neckline encircled by pearl buttons, long, sheer, pointed sleeves that snap at the wrists, and a concealed back zipper. The skirt falls elegantly from the high Basque-style waist. The tulle skirt lining peeks out at the bottom and offers an additional scalloped lace hem. The front of the skirt has a tiered layer of lace with a ruffled hem. Three additional tiers, done in tulle with scalloped lace trim, complete the front of the skirt.'"

Jana gave a long, wistful sigh. She looked up at Amy with wide eyes. "Mom, you have to get a dress just *exactly* like this when you get married."

When she got married. Ever since she was a little girl, she'd imagined so many different kinds of weddings. There was the hippy ceremony in Grandma Pearl's backyard. She'd be barefoot, wearing a dress of unbleached muslin and a crown of babies' breath on her head. Or she could choose the formal evening idea, featuring a gown of ivory silk with a long, long train trailing behind her, and Tracy, Robin, and every close friend she'd had since high school lining the platform in front of the church. There'd be candelabras at the front, satin bows at the end of each pew, and a live orchestra playing Pachelbel's Canon in D. The one she'd revisited most often, until she'd hit forty-five and decided marriage was not in God's plan for her life, was a simple ceremony in front of Grandma Pearl's fireplace. Tea-length dress, a sprig of lilies of the valley in her hair, a ring that had been in the groom's family for generations.

She winked at her daughter.

The back doorbell rang, and Amy got up and let Niesha in. After hugs all around, Niesha joined them at the table. Amy set a slice of icebox cake and a cup of tea in front of her. "Look what we just found." She pulled the bride book across the table and turned it so Niesha could see the pattern. "This was Violet's."

"The girl who went missing?"

"Yes." During one of their phone conversations, Amy had told Niesha about Violet. There were a lot of parallels between their younger years.

"It's gorgeous. Imagine..." Niesha let the word slide out on a wistful sigh.

"...need to find out the identity of the man in the estate sale picture," Abigail was saying as Amy refocused on the conversation at the other end of the table.

Tracy got up and retrieved a large envelope from her desk in the library. "Our evidence collection," she said, pouring out several pictures and the paper with the wedding guest list. She picked up the estate sale picture and set it on the table.

Aunt Abigail's forehead creased. "Have any of you shown this to anyone who might have known him?"

No one answered.

"How is Oriana Beecher doing?" Aunt Ruth asked.

Amy had tried to visit her friend Brooke's ninety-eight-year-old great-grandmother at least once a month since meeting her about eight months ago. She was due for a visit. "I'll check with Brooke. If Oriana is having a lucid day, maybe some of us could go to Harbor House and talk to her and Pop. There might be a few other people in assisted living who would recognize the man." She took out her phone and tapped on Brooke's name.

"Hi, Amy, long time no see." It had, in fact, been just over three hours since they'd hugged at church.

"Hi. Sorry to bother you on a Sunday. We found an old picture in Grandma Pearl's attic, and there's a guy in it we're trying to identify. I'd like to show it to your great-grandmother. How's she doing?" Brooke would know she was asking about more than her physical well-being.

"Gavin and I are heading over there in a few minutes. She sounded pretty clear on the phone a little while ago. Come on over."

"Would it overwhelm her if a bunch of the Allen women came to see her?" She looked around the table as she asked and received four nods. "We'll bring cake."

Brooke laughed. "That usually does the trick. I'll tell her you're coming."

"Great. We'd like to talk to Pop too."

"Oh, you know she'll love that."

"They're still an item, huh?" Amy smiled at the rest of the women at the table who had all heard the story of Oriana Beecher's eight-decade crush on the man who'd started Popelstopp's Popcorn Shop.

"Thick as thieves, as they say. I wouldn't be surprised if Pop popped the question any day now."

Though they joked about the romance between the centenarian and his two-year-younger sweetheart, Amy always got a bit misty-eyed seeing them together.

"We'll be there in about an hour."

"Okay," Brooke said. "I'll arrange enough chairs by the fireplace for all of us."

As Amy said goodbye, her gaze landed on the page Jana had just opened to in the bride book. Opposite a magazine cutout of a summer flower arrangement was a piece of notebook paper containing a handwritten wedding breakfast buffet. The paper wasn't attached to the page, so she picked it up and read through the menu out loud. "Chicken à la king, tomato aspic ring filled with avocado salad, finger sandwiches, peas with mushrooms, 24-hour-salad, butter-flake rolls, mixed nuts and bonbons, and, of course, cake."

"All but the aspic salad sounds yummy," Robin said. "Remember when Grandma made that gelatin with meat in it?"

Tracy's cheeks ballooned, and she clapped her palm over her mouth. "She made it with pigs' feet."

"And hard-boiled eggs and green peppers," Amy added, feeling as queasy as Tracy looked.

"Now you know how we suffered as children," Aunt Ruth said.

Aunt Abigail nodded. "But that was an economical meal in hard times. It was a great way to stretch leftovers."

"Maybe so," Amy said, "but I just remember staring at this jiggly mass of jelly with pieces of roast beef floating in it and running out…side." Her words slowed as she felt something under her thumb at the bottom of the page. Pushing her chair back, she stood and angled the paper toward the overhead light.

Faint impressions showed on the left side. Words, almost legible. "This must have been under another page she was writing on." She gasped as she made out one word, a name. "Thompson. It's a list of names." Goose bumps chased each other up and down her arms. "Can someone find a pencil, please? I think this piece of paper was under the wedding guest list. *Before* she crossed out one name with a vengeance."

Tracy handed her a pencil. Holding the pencil almost horizontal, Amy began to lightly shade the paper.

White loops and lines and dots began to appear until, after less than a minute, she was able to clearly read the list of names. Tracy held out the original paper so they could all see it. "There," she said, pointing first to the crossed-out name and then to the same spot on the page Amy had shaded.

Antoine and Sally Janvier

"That's the professor who verified the authenticity of the map Violet found." Aunt Ruth's voice was barely above a whisper. "Why would she cross his name out? And why did she do it with such fervor?"

Chapter Eleven

Pop and Oriana sat enthroned in wingback chairs in front of the fireplace at Harbor House. Oriana's small fingers were encased in Pop's large, gnarled hand that sported a massive gold ring encrusted with diamond chips surrounding an oval-cut purple stone. Oriana wore a lavender cable-knit sweater with pearls of the same shade. Her snow-white hair seemed to reflect her favorite color—favorite because of the ring on the hand holding hers. Her eyes—which sometimes looked distant, as if her mind was busy elsewhere, probably several decades past—appeared bright. At least for this window of time, she was present in the moment and there was no sign of the anger that sometimes took her captive.

The women took seats, and Amy handed a plastic container to Brooke. "Lemon lavender icebox cake."

Oriana raised her eyebrows. "Pearl's recipe?"

"Yes. You've had it before?"

"Oh my, yes. She made it for my baby shower. So delicious, and so pretty with all those layers. I had a small shower at the parsonage. No one wanted to make a big fuss, because they didn't approve of my husband. Of course, when Pearl had her first child"—Oriana lasered a darkening glare at Aunt Ruth—"every woman in town was invited and they put on the Ritz. Little mint cups that looked like baby buggies, four different kinds of cake, and all those silly games. Nothing was too good for Pearl. She always got everything she—"

"Doesn't this look delicious?" Brooke whipped the cover off the cake container and practically shoved it under Oriana's nose. "Can you smell the lavender?"

A sweet, peace-filled smile crinkled Oriana's cheeks. "Lovely. May we have some now? With a cup of tea?"

Brooke's shoulders sagged, and she let out a sigh the two elderly members of the circle wouldn't have been able to hear. Another crisis averted. "Coming right up. While I'm getting plates and tea, I think these ladies have an old photograph they'd like to show you. Maybe you can help them solve a mystery."

"Another mystery?" Pop asked. "You girls sure do lead exciting lives." His eyes glistened. "I wish Pearl could be here with us. She was so proud of all of you."

Oriana smiled up at him. "That's a wonderful idea. One of you should call Pearl. She made the cake, after all. Shouldn't she be here to enjoy it with us? Of course, she may not want to come if I'm here." As suddenly as the sun had seemed to break out in her countenance, it slipped back behind a cloud of bitterness.

While Tracy, Aunt Ruth, Robin, and Aunt Abigail all shared the same look of surprise and discomfort, Amy quickly pulled out the estate sale picture and crouched beside the elderly woman. By watching Brooke, she'd learned the art of distracting Oriana Beecher with something interesting or tasty. "Do either of you recognize this man?"

Oriana squinted. Pop took out a pair of reading glasses and slipped them on. After a moment he gave a slow nod. "Can't remember his name. He was a regular customer. In fact, he inspired one of our most popular popcorn flavors, French Provincial."

"Sounds more like furniture," Robin said.

Pop laughed. "Not the first time I've heard that. But have you tried it? Once you do, you won't be thinking of end tables. Tons of butter and our secret blend of marjoram, thyme, savory, basil, rosemary, sage, and fennel. Makes you think you're sitting on the banks of the Seine with a crusty loaf of bread. At least, that was our slogan when we came up with it back in the fifties."

"Sally's husband." Oriana's tone was flat.

Amy studied Oriana's expression. It was hard to tell if she was sad or angry. Maybe both. And then the name registered. "Sally? Sally Janvier? Is this Professor Janvier?"

Oriana nodded slowly. "Yes."

Brooke returned with a tray, and the women engaged Pop in conversation. As soon as he'd matched a name to the picture, pieces of memory seemed to fall into place. They told him about the name crossed off on the wedding guest list.

"He left everything behind for Sally. Home, family, friends," Pop said. "Everyone talked about their storybook romance, but it wasn't long before we started hearing rumors that life wasn't exactly paradise behind closed doors. Do you know Maura Childs?"

"Yes," Tracy said. "My husband works with her."

Pop nodded as he made the mental connection. "Maura was just a kid back then, but she had big ears. Figuratively, that is. Over the years she shared some things with my wife that I'm sure she picked up by eavesdropping." He looked around, as if assuring himself that Antoine Janvier was not lurking somewhere in the room. "Sally

Janvier was working at the bursar's office at the college when it was discovered that funds were going missing. Maura was sure Sally was the guilty one, that she'd been embezzling the money. I don't know if it was true or if she was ever caught."

"Hmm." Aunt Ruth's brow furrowed. "The young woman in that picture was our nanny, Violet Conway. Her father was—"

"Professor Conway." Once again, Pop appeared to be trying to reassemble bits and pieces of forgotten memories. "I knew Violet. Sweet girl. She was Professor Janvier's assistant for a while. I remember Maura telling my wife they'd had some kind of falling out." He waved a hand as if to erase his last words. "Sorry. I should not have brought that up when I don't have any facts. If you want the real story, talk to Maura."

Monday was World Kindness Day. On Friday, Amy had given each of her students three "compliment cards" for them to fill out. Each card had a student's name on it. Every child would write, and receive, three encouraging messages. This morning, she'd passed them out as soon as they'd settled in their seats. Now, halfway through the day, she was still amazed at the attitude of cooperation that prevailed. And the best was yet to come.

While they were at lunch, she covered the tables with clear plastic shower curtains she'd picked up at the dollar store and set out acrylic paint, brushes, and permanent markers. As they filed into the room, she complimented each one then asked them to get their art smocks out of their bins. When they were seated, she walked around the room with a bucket of smooth rocks, leaving two at each place.

Several hands shot in the air. She called on Annabelle.

"We're going to paint kindness rocks with kindness words on them, aren't we?"

"Yes, we are." Amy set the bucket on her desk and walked over to the whiteboard. "Let's make a list of sayings that will encourage people. Things like 'Have a nice day.' Call them out, not too loud, and I'll write them down."

Letting them break the "One person talking at a time," rule was a little kindness gift she'd give to her class—just this once.

"You can do it!"

"You're smart!"

"Be kind!"

"Kindness rocks!" This one got a round of laughter.

"Peace."

"Love."

"Smile!"

"It works best if you paint the whole rock one color and let it dry before decorating it with your words and whatever pictures you choose. Flowers, sunshine, hearts, maybe a smiley face. When you're finished, wash up and take a book to the reading corner." When she gave them the go-ahead to start, the room fell quiet.

While neon colors, rainbows, flowers, and polka-dots transformed the rocks, Amy sat at her desk, catching up on grading papers until she heard giggling from the table with the highest percentage of troublemakers. She got up and walked over to stand behind James and Brian. On one rock sprawled a surprisingly lifelike tarantula. A wide-mouth shark, blood dripping from one tooth, covered the other. They were in the process of building a catapult out of pencils and rubber bands for their other two rocks, both painted black.

Amy had learned a few tricks in a quarter-century of teaching. "Great job, boys. I'd like you to take them down to the office and show them to Principal Walker and tell her why you chose these designs to celebrate World Kindness Day."

Oh, for a camera at a time like this. Two pale faces stared up at her. She stared back until Brian said, "I think I'll paint a daisy. And balloons. Everybody likes balloons." James followed with, "Yeah, maybe I'll make a sunflower, and stars."

Amy smiled, turned around, and returned to her seat. When she reached the bottom of the stack of worksheets, she sent a text to Miles, knowing he might not see it for hours.

IF YOU ARE FREE ON SATURDAY AFTERNOON, WOULD YOU AND YOUR KIDS AND YOUR BOAT LIKE TO JOIN US (JUST ABOUT MY ENTIRE FAMILY!) ON THE RIVER? JEFF, CHAD, AND KEVIN WANT TO DIVE TO SEARCH THE PLACE WHERE JOSH FOUND THE BOARD AND THE PURSE.

Thirty seconds later, her screen lit with his answer, a GIF of the chief of police in the movie *Fargo* saying, "You betcha. Yeah."

Amy stifled a laugh at the rest of his message.

DID I EVER TELL YOU ABOUT THE SHIPWRECK DIVE I DID IN 2009? THAT'LL BE THE TOPIC FOR OUR NEXT DINNER DATE. I KNOW IT'S ONLY LIKE 10 OR 12 FEET DEEP WHERE WE'LL BE SEARCHING, BUT I'LL BRING SCUBA GEAR AND MY UNDERWATER METAL DETECTOR. AND MY NEW AKASO BRAVE 4 PRO 4K30 ACTION WATERPROOF CAMERA.

She could imagine him grinning and practically vibrating with anticipation. "Men," she said out loud. Deep down, most of them were still first-grade boys.

"Come on in."

The diminutive art history professor, Maura Childs, was dwarfed by the massive oak desk she sat behind. The woman had been a part of the college her whole life. Surely she would have some answers for them.

Amy settled into a leather chair across the desk from Maura. "I'm wondering what you can tell me about Professor Antoine Janvier."

"Hmm." Maura leaned back. "What do you want to know?"

Amy filled her in on what they knew about Violet and *River Dancer*.

"I haven't thought of Violet in years. Such a nice girl. She was four or five years older than me, but I always liked her because she treated me like an equal. Did you know your grandmother asked me to spy on her?"

Amy raised her eyebrows. "I did not know that. Why?"

"I'm not really sure. I guess I had a reputation for being an eavesdropper and a bit too interested in everybody's business. I think I was the perfect candidate for snooping around after Violet. I assumed some boy was bothering her, but I never saw anything worrisome. Well, other than the time when I was invited to a tea in one of the women's dorms. I was walking back from the bathroom, and I saw Violet talking on the phone in the common room. I thought it very odd she'd be using it, since she didn't live on campus. I tried to get close, but all I could tell was that she was very angry."

Leaning forward, Amy tried not to appear too pushy. "Can you remember anything she said? A name maybe?"

The fold lines on Maura's forehead deepened. "I don't remember the exact words, but she said she had proof and insisted the person talk to the authorities. I don't know who she was talking to, but she was adamant that if the person didn't do it, she would."

Had Violet witnessed something? Did she disappear because someone needed to silence her?"

"Do you even know if she's still alive?" Maura asked.

"Sadly, no."

"When I was a sophomore, I was allowed to skip one of my high school classes and sit in on one of Professor Conway's history classes. When he talked about the Civil War, he brought Violet in to show a quilt she'd made by hand out of raw cotton, just like enslaved women would have. It was stunning. Come to think of it, I'm pretty sure it's still here in our archive room, along with everything else that was cleared out of her father's office." She rested the tip of one index finger against the side of her nose. "There were so many rumors flying around about what happened to her, and I had my own questions about whether it was connected to what her father was doing before he passed."

"What was he doing?"

"Keep in mind that I had the overactive imagination of a fifteen-year-old, but I'm sure he was hiding something." Maura removed her glasses and ran both hands over her face. Her narrow shoulders rose and fell. "Professor Conway was a bit of the stereotypical eccentric professor. One of those eccentricities was his habit of talking to himself. I worked at the college three days a week after school. I was what I suppose you'd call a gofer. I did whatever I was asked, from emptying wastebaskets to filing, cleaning, or running papers from one building or floor to another. It was a job tailor-made for an overly curious teenager. As I was in and out of offices, I often picked up bits and pieces of Professor Conway's conversations with himself. One day, when I was in an adjoining storeroom, his door was slightly ajar and I overheard what sounded like plans for some kind of an expedition. He talked about needing an axe, a sword, rope, even a bottle of rum. My insatiable curiosity was piqued, so I snuck close enough to peek in. He was hunched over a card table in the middle of his office, intently studying something that covered almost the entire top of the table. I couldn't get a good look, but from where I stood, it appeared to be an old map."

"Like a treasure map?" Should she tell Maura what she knew?

"More like something you might see in a children's book about pirates, but I very much doubt that's what it was. Maps with 'X marks the spot' are all fictitious. Robert Louis Stevenson got the idea for writing *Treasure Island* after he and his son drew a map of an imaginary island while they were on holiday in Scotland in the summer of 1881. In a letter to a friend a few months into writing it, he said, 'If this don't fetch the kids, why, they have gone rotten since my day.'" Maura held up one arthritic hand. "Sorry, lecturing is my primary language."

Amy chuckled. "No apologies needed. I love hearing where authors get their ideas. *Treasure Island* certainly did 'fetch' kids. I remember reading it when I was ten, and now my son is hooked on it. Fancies himself a swashbuckler."

Maura laughed. "Ah, to be young and free to spend your days in fantasy."

"So true. You said the map looked old. Can you describe it?"

"It was tan, and the edges were curled in spots. I don't think it was drawn on paper. Some kind of cloth."

"Animal skin?" Amy asked the question without thinking. Now she'd have to explain it. "We heard from someone else that Professor Conway had an old map that might have been drawn on a tanned hide."

"Could be. There were shapes drawn on it. I wasn't close enough to tell if they were continents or islands or what. Sorry I'm not more help. Whatever it was, I gathered he planned on going there and was making a list of everything he'd need for living in the wilderness. I will say it surprised me. He walked with a limp, and I'd heard him complain to Professor Janvier about back pain that kept him from sleeping. A war injury, from what I understood. And he had a veritable pharmacy of pills and sprays for seasonal allergies. Professor Conway was definitely not the outdoorsy, adventurous type. The whole thing was just plain strange."

Amy rubbed her forearms. Did Violet's father really die of natural causes, or could he have been killed because of the treasure map?

"He and Antoine Janvier were friends," Amy said. "And we know there was some kind of conflict between Professor Janvier and Violet while she was planning her wedding. Any idea what that could have been about?"

"Professor Janvier got along with everyone. Everyone except the woman he was married to. I can't imagine anyone having a conflict with him." Maura's expression became pensive. "I did overhear one conversation between him and Violet while I spied on her for your grandmother. They were in his classroom. She said she was quitting because, even though she knew it would hurt him, she had to do what was right. I thought she was quitting school, even though it wasn't long before graduation, and I remember admiring her, thinking I wanted to have that kind of integrity and conviction when I got to be her age." Maura looked down at her desk. "Maybe it was that conviction that cost her her life."

Chapter Twelve

"Mom? Are you awake?"

The hesitant whisper broke into Amy's dream of floating down the Huzzah River in a rubber tube without a care in the world, like she'd done so often before becoming a foster mom. She lifted her sleep mask, opened one eye, and blinked at Jana, who was dressed in jeans, a hoodie, and high-top tennis shoes. "It's Saturday, honey. Why are you up so early?"

"It's nine o'clock."

"No." Amy shot straight up and whipped the mask across the bed. Whirling around so fast the room spun for a moment, she looked at the clock, not believing what she was seeing. She hadn't slept past seven since… She couldn't remember the last time. She grabbed her phone, unplugged it, and unlocked the screen. She gaped at the list of texts and calls she'd missed. Her nighttime "do not disturb" was still set to stop at seven thirty. Had she actually slept through a ringing phone? "I'm sorry, honey. Did you and Matt get breakfast?"

Jana nodded. "We had peanut butter and honey sandwiches."

"Good. I'm so glad you can take care of yourselves."

"We've had a lot of practice." Matt stood in the doorway. The excitement that had kept him jabbering about the boat ride last night was nowhere to be found.

Was he referring to the years before they came to live with her, when their drug-dependent biological mother was often passed out or gone? Or did he mean the last few weeks? She wouldn't ask. "I'm so sorry."

"Dr. Miles and Colton and Natalie are downstairs." His somber voice matched his expression.

Amy jumped out of bed. "Tell them I'll be right down. Go… entertain them. Offer him coffee."

"He already finished it."

No. No. No. This couldn't be happening. They were meeting the rest of her family at nine fifteen. She ran into the bathroom. Just before slamming the door harder than she needed to, she caught a glimpse of Matt's face. He wasn't only disappointed. He was embarrassed.

What memories did this awaken for him? Having to get up and fix breakfast for his little sister because his mother wasn't functional.

Tears stung as she brushed her teeth. No time for makeup. Or a needed shower.

A running commentary of excuses ricocheted in her head as she tossed clothes onto the bed. It had been a busier than usual week. The appointment with Maura, a second meeting for the Pop's Place fundraiser, a haircut on Wednesday, dentist appointments for the kids on Thursday after school, late nights writing content for her website and revising and scanning old worksheets. The coming week would be different.

Would it? She had a phone interview with a local radio station on Monday afternoon to promote the fundraiser. That was also the day she'd start putting teasers on social media sites aimed at teachers. Niesha had given her specific things to post each day, strategically

Nothing Gold Can Stay

timed to drum up excitement leading up to Cyber Monday, which, according to Niesha and several online sites she'd checked, would be the most optimal launch day for her website and Etsy store. And then there was rehearsal for the fashion show and… Amy grabbed a hooded sweatshirt and closed the bedroom door behind her, symbolically shutting all of her to-dos inside. They would all be waiting for her when she returned. For now, she would be present in the moment. With a deep breath and a quick prayer for strength, she headed down the stairs.

Seventy-one degrees and sunny. The trees lining the river were in full glory. It was her favorite season. Why couldn't it last longer? Amy leaned back on the seat cushion in Miles's boat and closed her eyes. A Robert Frost poem her mother had loved came to mind.

> *Nature's first green is gold,*
> *Her hardest hue to hold.*
> *Her early leaf's a flower;*
> *But only so an hour.*
> *Then leaf subsides to leaf.*
> *So Eden sank to grief,*
> *So dawn goes down to day.*
> *Nothing gold can stay.*

The verses had always made her feel melancholy, a reminder that nothing good lasts forever. When Grandma Pearl had suggested putting the poem on the obituary cards for her parents' funeral, Amy had hated the idea…until her grandmother sat her down and showed her another way to look at it. "What 'nothing gold can stay' says to me is that we shouldn't hang on too tightly to the things around us. There will be hard seasons of letting go, but God always brings the new leaf. These words give me reason to hope."

Today she heard the hope in those words. Today it felt as if God smiled down on their expedition.

She waved at the filled-to-capacity pontoon boat. Robin, Terry, Kai, Tracy, Jeff, Kevin, and Chad led the way. There was something symbolic about being in a separate boat with Miles and their four children. Separate, yet still a part of the family, this circle of people who genuinely cared. Cared enough to tell her, "You have to slow down or you're going to crash."

Tracy had said the words when they'd arrived at the river fifteen minutes late, and she'd given her litany of excuses, but it had still hurt. Because they were true. Her answer to her sister played through her brain as she sat soaking up the sun's rays. "I will. It'll all be behind me soon." Just a few more days to push through with little sleep and a smile pasted on her face. And then… Then she'd give her kids her full attention for the best Christmas ever.

Unless her Etsy site was a huge success and she needed to keep creating new content. Or it wasn't a huge success and she needed to find another way to raise money for their vacation. The word "dream" in dream vacation had begun tarnishing the past few days. Was this really what her kids wanted? Was it really what she wanted?

Nothing gold can stay. Was she hanging on too tightly to her dream of Golden Sky Dude Ranch?

"A Hershey's kiss for your thoughts." Miles, sitting behind the wheel, held out a bag of silver-wrapped chocolates.

"Breakfast of lazy moms," she said, her stomach growling as she took one. "I'm really sorry about this morning."

"Your punishment has already been meted out. You can quit being penitent." He winked at her. Jeff had told her the penalty for tardiness was buying them all coffee when they got off the river. One hand on the wheel, Miles turned and stared at her with a look that seemed to pierce her soul. "I'm worried about you."

"I'm fine. Just a little…" She wasn't sure how to finish the sentence. Stressed? Exhausted? Overcommitted, stretched thin, unable to say no, pulled in way too many directions? "I'm just a little tired."

"It's affecting Matt and Jana, Amy." The amusement that had danced in his eyes moments ago was gone.

"I know." Her voice was barely above a whisper. "I just have to get through the end of the month, and then we'll all be okay."

Miles slowed the motor when the other boat stopped. Was this it? The place Josh had described? Her heart rate sped up as the boat came to a stop. Miles pointed to the anchor sitting next to her feet, and she jumped up and hefted it over the side. Miles gave her a nod of approval and then reached out and took her hand. "Do you have plans for tonight?"

"No. I mean, we're not going anywhere. But I've got a couple of hours of work to do. I just found a file of worksheets I used when I taught a unit on the elements of a story. I need to tweak them a bit and make a clean copy, and I have to work on my costume for Tuesday night and talk to Niesha about—"

Miles held up one hand, stopping the gush of words. "We, the six of us, are going out for dinner and a movie tonight. A nice, fun, distracting night. We'll pick you up at six. No talk of bridal showers or fundraisers or Etsy stores or missing people. Or boats. And no argument. Doctor's orders."

She nodded and was about to answer with a thank-you when Kai yelled, "This is it! We're here!"

Matt stood, camera at the ready. Amy studied him. She'd tried several times to talk to him about what was going on at school, but each time he'd answered with "Nothing." This was not like her son. Something was definitely not right.

Before scooting out the door this morning, she'd said, "We need a videographer for this expedition. Go grab your video camera." He'd looked down at his shoes. "I…left it at school."

Before she had a chance to question him, he'd flown up the stairs. Moments later he'd returned with her old Canon that she'd given him a few months earlier. "Still pictures are just as good," he'd said, a smile on his face she could tell he didn't feel.

They sat in silence as the men in the pontoon boat, already wearing wetsuits, put on air tanks. One by one, they slid into the water.

Miles pointed to the depth gauge on his dash panel. "Fourteen feet right here." Instead of jumping up to put on his own diving gear, he swiveled his seat to face her. "What are you hoping to find?"

"Anything," was the first answer that came to mind. "Josh is sure the board hanging in River Dan's was sawed off. That says intentional destruction. If we could find anything else that confirmed that, we'd know we were looking at a crime scene. I know that sounds dramatic, but it would give us a direction. If Josh is wrong and what he found was pieces left after an accident, then I'm scared of what we might find. If Violet's purse was here, then..." She stared at the murky water, wishing for something to appear. Something other than what they all feared. "I just hope we don't find—"

Her next words evaporated as one of the men broke the surface.

Jeff took out his mouthpiece, slid his face mask onto his forehead, and then heaved something heavy into Kai's waiting hands.

"It's...metal. And melted. Half melted." Kai grabbed a rag and rubbed the surface of the shapeless mass until sunlight glinted on a bit of shiny gold. "I see the word 'River.' I think..." He jumped to his feet, holding the object over his head. "It's *River Dancer*'s bell!"

June 17, 1955

It's almost midnight, and I'm exhausted. I wasn't going to write tonight. I don't want to revisit this horrible day. But then I realized that recording every single detail might reveal something Howard and I, or the police, have missed.

Violet disappeared today, and so did our boat. We have no idea where they are. The only clue we have is a broken window. Half the windowpane is busted out, shattered on the floor in her room. The opening is not large enough for her to get out or anyone to get in. We searched the room but couldn't find the object that someone must have hurled through the window, and I can't imagine why we didn't hear it. Her purse is not hanging on the hook behind her bedroom door where she always puts it, and I found splatters of tea and black ink smudges on her desk. Her room is always spotless, so that's strange, but it doesn't appear that anything was ransacked, and all of our doors were still locked.

Howard talked to Lenny as soon as we realized she was gone. He was beside himself with worry. When the police went to his apartment, he wasn't home, and we haven't been able to reach him again. The police suggested the two of them may have planned this together. They think Vi may have taken the boat and met him somewhere later, maybe eloping. They say they will keep a lookout, but I can tell they don't believe this is anything more than two young people taking off on a weekend getaway. But that makes no sense. They could have done that with our blessing, and we would have let them borrow the boat for their honeymoon. That can't be it. They were both so excited about planning their wedding. It was the one bright spot in Vi's life right now.

Officer Miller tried to assure us they will probably be back before Lenny has to be at work on Monday, but they don't know them like we do. They are both able to captain the boat and have taken it out with friends before, but they would never take it without our permission. Something is very, very wrong here, and I want to scream because no one is taking us seriously.

I feel so guilty. I've been so busy lately that I haven't had time to just sit and listen to Violet. I know she's been upset. The estate sale last week was traumatizing for her. Living in a house that still contains so many of my parents' prized possessions, I can't even begin to imagine what it must have felt like to watch people greedily carry away the precious things that surrounded her all her life. Why, why, why wasn't I more attentive?

Saturday, June 18, 1955

Howard interrupted my writing last night by handing me a note he found under the telephone. It's in Vi's handwriting, and it is unfinished, ending in the middle of a word. All it says is:

Howard and Pearl, I am so sorry. I didn

Chapter Thirteen

Amy checked her phone when they got home from their treasure-hunting expedition. Niesha had sent a picture of herself standing in front of a full-length mirror, wearing a white dress that came to her knees. With a circle of white flowers on her head, she looked stunning. Her message read, WHAT DO YOU THINK? I WORE THIS TO A SCHOOL FUNCTION LAST YEAR. IS IT BRIDE-ISH ENOUGH?

Though the dress was lovely, Amy felt a moment of disappointment for Niesha. She was hoping Niesha would call Whitney, who would have given her a great deal on a secondhand dress. Her first thought was to offer to take her to Pop Rocks Vintage. *When?* Common sense took over, and she held up both hands—a sign of surrender. Niesha was a big girl. If she was happy with this dress, Amy would be happy for her.

Jana walked in and sat beside her. Amy snuggled her close and showed her the picture. "This is Niesha's wedding dress. Isn't it pretty?"

"Yeah. But aren't brides supposed to wear long dresses?"

And there went her resolve. If she called Whitney now, they could find a time to pick out some dresses. Maybe she'd even open up the store tomorrow. Amy could pick up Niesha and—

Know when to say no.

She was about to argue with the intrusive thought but took a deep breath instead. "Lots of brides wear long dresses, and lots wear short ones. Some brides get married in jeans and T-shirts." Jana's shocked expression made her laugh. "It's just important that every bride wears what makes her comfortable and happy."

"I guess. But I'm going to wear a loooong dress with a loooong veil and carry lots and lots of white flowers."

"I can't wait to be there. Actually, no, I can wait. I want to keep you this size for a long time."

Jana giggled. "Just till I'm eight. But I won't get married until I'm like seventeen."

Amy kissed the top of her daughter's head. "How about twenty-seven?" She took the phone back and typed a reply.

VERY BRIDE-ISH. THE DRESS, AND YOU, ARE BEAUTIFUL.

"That's a nice thing to say," Jana said, sliding off the bed. "Can I go watch *Pirate Dog* again? I just love, love, love Scrappy."

"Go, my scrappy girl. But be sure you're ready to go in an hour."

After showering, Amy slipped into the flannel robe her mother had bought her before she left for college. Old, thin, worn in spots, it felt like a hug from her mom. She could sure use one right now.

She sat on the edge of her bed as she brushed her wet hair. She had less than an hour to clear her mind before Miles and his kids came to pick them up. She grabbed the devotional book she hadn't had time to read earlier. The book was arranged by topic. Though she'd been reading through from cover to cover, she decided to look in the table of contents for something relevant. She smiled when she found one titled "Taming the Busy Beast." She read it through then grabbed a highlighter and marked a few statements she'd need to return to.

> *Your body and soul were not created for hurry and being overly busy. Being too busy has the power to rob you of what is most important in life.*
>
> *Some of us live as though we are unaware there are alternatives to a too-fast, overbusy life.*
>
> *Start by defining why you feel the need to crowd your to-do list. Many of us have the false belief that doing more and doing it faster will make us "more."*

Above empty lines at the bottom of the page, it said, "In the space below, describe what is most important to you. Then be honest—how do hurry and busyness help or hurt your quest for these things?"

She didn't have time to write, but she knew the answers. She said them out loud in a prayer. "Lord, I want to be closer to You and to the people I love. Hurry and busyness create distance. Help me slow down and say no to anything that distracts me from those goals."

She stood and walked into the hallway. Matt was in his room, sitting on his bed, head bent over the camera he'd used to take pictures of their time on the river. A good place to start.

"Get some good ones?" she asked.

He nodded.

"Can I see?" Not waiting for an answer, she sat next to him.

He handed her the camera. She scrolled through the pictures, commenting on his eye for capturing action shots and facial expressions. "Let's get these on my laptop tomorrow so you can see them better."

Again, he answered with a nod.

"Matt, I need you to tell me what's going on." She crooked her finger under his chin and lifted it so he had no choice but to look at her.

"Why would somebody hurt a person like Violet?" he asked. "Aunt Ruth said she was really nice."

She lowered her hand, knowing the deeper question wasn't really about Violet. Amy shot up a quick prayer for wisdom. "My grandma used to say, 'Hurt people hurt people.' It's kind of like what happens when you line up dominoes and then push the first one."

"Do you think she knew somebody wanted to hurt her?"

"I don't know. Maybe. We aren't absolutely sure someone kidnapped her, but if they did, she might have known she had an enemy. Are you wondering if she could have done something to stop it?"

"Yes."

"Well, in her case, she probably should have gone to the police. The people who might have taken her were probably very dangerous. But there are a lot of times when someone hurts us that we can at least try going out of our way to be kind to them. Remember a few months ago when we read in the book of Romans about how we should treat an enemy?"

Matt's brow furrowed, and then the slightest of smiles made his eyes dance. "The thing about heaping coals of burning fire on his head."

Amy reached out and ruffled his hair. "Do you remember the rest of it?"

"We're supposed to feed our enemies if they're hungry."

"Right." She reached for the Bible that sat on his nightstand under an empty soda can and a comic book. When she'd found the passage in Romans chapter twelve, she set the Bible on his lap. "Read seventeen through twenty-one."

"'Do not repay anyone evil for evil. Be careful to do what is right in the eyes of everyone. If it is possible, as far as it depends on you, live at peace with everyone. Do not take revenge, my dear friends, but leave room for God's wrath, for it is written: "It is mine to avenge; I will repay," says the Lord. On the contrary: "If your enemy is hungry, feed him; if he is thirsty, give him something to drink. In doing this, you will heap burning coals on his head. Do not be overcome by evil, but overcome evil with good.'"

Matt sat still for a moment, as if letting the words sink in, then he looked up, eyes glistening with unshed tears. "Lucas Cartwright stole my video camera."

"Oh, honey. Did you tell anyone? One of your teachers?"

"No. He'd just do something else. Something worse."

"Okay. I won't step in yet if you think you can handle this yourself. But I need some details. Start with how you found out he took it."

"I set it down on my chair when I emptied my tray after lunch. Two guys started arguing really loud and I turned to watch, and when I went to get my camera, it was gone. Nobody saw who took it, but later Koby said he saw Lucas using it on his bus."

Amy wanted to wrap her arms around him, to kiss away the hurt, but Miles was right. This was something she couldn't swoop in and fix.

"Do you think he took it just because he wanted it, or because it was yours?"

"Because it's mine." No hesitation. Matt was sure about this. He scrubbed both hands over his face. "A couple weeks ago we had a hoops contest in gym, sixth graders against seventh. It got down to me against Lucas, and I won. Since then he's been calling me dumb names and laughing at me."

"Why do you think he feels the need to do that?"

"I think his dad is really mean to him." He closed his eyes for a few seconds. "I guess I should try the being nice to your enemy thing."

"That would be a good place to start, but be careful. If you're going to talk to him, don't do it alone. Maybe at lunch when lots of people are around. And maybe have Colton right by your side and—" She stopped and then laughed. "Sorry. It's a mom thing. I just want to make it better."

Matt nodded then leaned his shoulder against hers. "That's okay. I'm glad I have a mom who wants to."

Doctor's orders. A nice, fun, distracting night. Dinner and a movie—the movie she'd promised the kids they would see together. Would she have followed through if Miles hadn't planned it? Amy sighed as she stood in front of the full-length mirror that hung on the back of her closet door, fumbling with red hoop earrings. She wore one of the outfits Whitney had put together for her. Faded-just-right jeans that flared below the knee. Bright red pullover, black-and-white houndstooth-print scarf, nubby gray cardigan, and short black boots. All secondhand. All far more stylish than anything she would have assembled on her own. So why wasn't she feeling it?

She glanced at the reflection of the pile of cloth on her bed. She'd chosen to model the yoke dress for the fashion show. Using the picture of Violet, she'd cut out two giant white blobs from a bed sheet and two bright yellow circles from felt and was in the process of stitching them by hand to a pale yellow jumper Aunt Ruth had found in the back of her closet. She'd planned on getting it done tonight, but...doctor's orders.

Miles meant well, she knew that, but didn't he realize his distraction plan meant she'd be up even later than usual tonight? It also meant she'd be working on Sunday, something she usually tried not to do.

"They're here!" Matt called up the stairs. He'd peeked in a few minutes ago, asking if he could have a granola bar before they left. She knew it was only an excuse to check up on her, to make sure she was ready to go. Just a few more days. Her family couldn't fall apart in such a short time. Could it?

Once again, she closed the door, leaving all of her clamoring coulda-shoulda-wouldas behind. She lifted her chin as she walked down the stairs, where Miles stood eyeing her with an approving smile.

They got in the Jeep, Amy in the passenger seat, the two girls in the middle, and the boys, by choice, in the "way back." When Miles started the vehicle, a song Amy loved was just ending. She closed her eyes as she listened to the words coming from the speaker in front of her. The last stanza, about being still and knowing God heard prayer, always gave her a sense of calm. Something she needed at the moment.

The next song had the opposite effect. As a song about slowing down played, her pulse sped up. If she didn't know better, she'd think Miles had created a playlist just for her. But he wasn't that kind of person.

"Kind of fitting, isn't it?" Miles reached over and laid his hand on top of hers.

Not trusting her voice, she simply nodded.

"Where are we going to eat?" Colton yelled.

"It's a surprise." Miles winked at him in the rearview mirror.

They sat in silence for the next ten minutes. Silent except for the songs on the radio and the kids talking in the back seats. Amy stared out the side window as they crossed the Mississippi. The sight of the wide river usually lifted her spirits, no matter what mood she was in, but in spite of sunlight sparking like diamonds on the water, it wasn't working today. The conviction brought on by the song and the well-meaning words from Tracy and Miles earlier in the day felt like a weight on her chest.

When Miles flipped the turn signal before they got off the bridge, Matt shouted, "I know where we're going! Yes! You're gonna love it, Colton."

River Dan's.

Her initial reaction was irritation. Tonight was supposed to be a distraction, time away from thinking and talking about things like bridal showers and Etsy...and missing people and boats. But he'd brought her here?

This morning, after Jeff had found the partially melted bell, Miles had jumped in with his metal detector, and they'd spent the next two hours combing the shoreline around the oak tree. They'd filled two mesh bags with their finds. Because of "doctor's orders," they wouldn't have time to fully examine their haul until after church tomorrow. And Miles thought he could bring her here and she wouldn't talk about it?

Maybe it was being on the edge of exhaustion, but it suddenly struck her as funny.

Dan Jordan stood next to the hostess station when they walked in. "Nice to see you again, Amy. Are you here for dinner, or the boat mystery?"

"Just dinner." Miles answered for her, giving her a playful nudge. "No talk of mysteries tonight."

Amy nodded toward Matt, who was pointing out the *River Dan* board to Colton. "That's what he thinks."

As Dan showed them to their booth, the boys kept up a running commentary about the demise of *River Dancer*. "I still think it was pirates," Matt said. "I looked up modern-day pirates. These days, pirates have AK-47s and machine guns and rocket launchers. They even use night-vision goggles and GPS devices. Sometimes they take hostages and demand a ransom. One time, pirates attacked a big cruise ship, but the ship's crew scared them away with an L-RAD machine. That's short for long-range acoustic device. It's like a supersonic sound wave cannon that can destroy a person's—"

Amy interrupted the supersonic weapons lesson with a hand on Matt's shoulder. "Why don't you and Jana tell Colton and Natalie about the Shipwreck Sundae?"

While the kids took off their jackets, Amy pulled Miles aside. "I talked to Matt before you picked us up."

"Did *he* talk?"

"Yes." She gave him a quick summary. "I'm glad you warned me to step back. I was ready to charge in like an angry mama bear, but this might just be a huge life lesson."

Miles slid his arm around her. "We make a pretty good team."

"We do, don't we?"

Chapter Fourteen

On Sunday, Amy stood under the archway leading to the library at Jeff and Tracy's, staring at the bits and pieces of what had once been *River Dancer*. A sense of sadness mingled with curiosity. Would all of this tell them anything?

They hadn't yet taken everything out of the mesh bags, but Jeff estimated they'd retrieved over forty pounds of metal, including two brass clamshell scoop vents, a propeller plate with "Chris Craft" still legible, the bow plate, fuel caps, three propeller blades, and various engine parts Amy couldn't begin to name.

The far end of the table was filled with pieces of wood, all weathered and splintered and showing signs of charring. There was no denying now that *River Dancer* had been partially destroyed by fire. But that fact only raised more questions. Was it fire that caused its original demise? Engine fire? Lightning strike? Or had someone set the boat on fire to cover evidence? And evidence of what? Theft? Abduction? Or worse?

"Too bad we didn't find any—" Matt clamped his lips tight when Amy shot him a silencing look. Everyone in the room knew he was about to say "bones."

She was thankful they hadn't yet found any evidence of Violet's fate. Knowing that Violet's sunflower purse had probably been buried at the same time as the name board of *River Dancer* was disturbing, but not conclusive. Like everything else, it stirred up more confusion. If someone was trying to hide evidence, why wasn't Violet's purse the first thing thrown into the blaze? Though nothing was readable now, her purse must have contained a driver's license and pictures that could have been identifiable at the time. Wouldn't the culprit have wanted to obliterate anything that would trace back to her?

They needed answers. What happened to Violet Conway? Had she run away, or left against her will? Was she still alive?

"Hey." Miles gripped something square, about half the size of his hand. "Look at this."

In the center of the tarnished metal was a hole. A keyhole. Made for a skeleton key.

Amy gasped, darted into the kitchen, and retrieved the key they'd found in Violet's purse. She held it up to the keyhole in the piece of metal Miles held out.

"It's too small."

Miles shrugged. "Well, it was worth a try." His smile washed over her.

Terry pulled something out of a bag. "Cool." He held up two cursive letters, *Cr*, that had probably once been shiny chrome and part of "Chris Craft."

The timer on Tracy's stove buzzed, and Amy walked into the kitchen to check on the scalloped potatoes. She opened the oven door. Not quite the golden-brown top she was waiting for. She reset the timer. While she waited, she took her phone out of her purse, where she'd told herself she would leave it all day.

Last night, after an amazing day, she'd stayed up late to work on new entries for her Etsy store, finally getting to bed after one. This morning, feeling groggy but determined, she'd sent Niesha a message: Taking a real sabbath rest today. Notifications off! Niesha had answered: You go girl! If I send you anything it's just because I don't want to forget it. Ignore until Monday.

Ignore. She shouldn't even unlock the screen. But what if...?

Two missed calls from Niesha, and three text messages. One from Carrie. Sorry to interrupt your Sunday. Tell me your thoughts on these bridal shower cake pictures. If you can pick one and call me today, that would be great. I might need to order a couple of things to get them on time.

The next one was from Niesha. I know I told you to ignore my messages, but this is really, really important. I contacted a college friend who has a huge following on Instagram. She's doing a big push for women-owned businesses this week and wants to feature yours, but she needs to know if you're in by four o'clock today.

Amy leaned against the counter and pressed her forearms to her middle. She could ignore the group message from Whitney. Except for the fact that the first word was Urgent!

I just talked to a young mom who was living with a boyfriend but got kicked out. I'm in St. Louis until late tonight, so I can't do her intake interview and show her around. Is anyone available?

Amy's shoulders rose to her ears. This was a legitimate need, an unselfish request. She had people to watch the kids. There was no reason she couldn't say yes to Whitney's request.

Except that she'd made a promise to herself to start saying no, to not put anything more on that overfull plate.

A bubbling sound from the oven pulled her attention back to the here and now, and she grabbed two potholders and opened the oven. Perfect. At least one thing was going right. She grabbed the sides of the Pyrex pan. The timer buzzed, and she jumped. Her right hand smacked against the top element. She yelped, and unwanted tears sprang to her eyes. She blinked hard to force them away, but when a pair of arms engulfed her, she shattered, falling against Aunt Abigail's shoulder with heaving sobs. "I…can't…do…this. I'm a horrible mom, and I'm letting everyone down, and nothing is getting done like I want it to, and…"

"Shh." Aunt Abigail rubbed her back. "How about if you and I go sit in the study and have a little chat? I've got a few things I've been meaning to talk to you about anyway."

Great. All she needed was another lecture about getting her priorities straight. What did her aunt who'd never had children know about disappointing them and feeling like a failure as a mom? Bracing herself, she followed Aunt Abigail down the hall to the study and sat on one end of the love seat. Aunt Abigail flipped the wall switch, starting a blaze in the gas fireplace, and sat on the other end. "Have I ever told you why I never married?"

This was not the conversation starter Amy had expected. Was she finally going to get some answers? "No." She sniffled and blew her nose, and then she gave Aunt Abigail her full attention.

"It may have come from being the middle child. Ruthy was the achiever, the smart one, and your daddy was the cute, outgoing one. Growing up, I always felt I had something to prove. You'd think that would have changed when I became an adult, but it didn't. In college, I took more credits than any of my friends and still got involved in my sorority and volunteering as a Big Sister.

"After college, I got my dream job with a travel agency in Grand Rapids that sent me all over the world. On one of those transatlantic flights, I met a woman whose passion for Jesus was contagious. She reminded me of my mother. My faith had become stagnant, but when I landed back in the States, I jumped in with both feet. I got involved with a group of Jesus People and, besides working full-time, I did street ministry, joined the worship team, and started mentoring teen girls. Two years later, I met a man who was everything I didn't even know I was looking for. Gentle, handsome, funny, a vibrant Christian. I fell hard. His goal was to buy a farm and turn it into a retreat center for missionaries. He started searching for property in Northern Michigan and wanted me to help him, but I couldn't get away. I had so many obligations to so many people—all good things—that I couldn't find time to support his dream."

Aunt Abigail turned toward the window, a faraway look in her eyes. "On one of those trips, he fell asleep at the wheel and hit a tree. He died later that day. The guilt almost buried me. I was sure that if I'd been with him, it wouldn't have happened. Or if I hadn't been at a meeting, his parents could have reached me and I could have gotten to the hospital before he died. I spent a lot of years wallowing in regret." Her gaze latched on to Amy's. Her message needed no words. Amy heard it loud and clear. *Don't let that happen to you.*

"I'm so sorry." Amy's voice, rough and raw, sounded strange to her ears.

"Sadly, I coped with my guilt by throwing myself into even more busyness. I think part of me wanted to make sure I'd never have the chance to fall in love again and ruin someone else's life. Even though it was my choice to remain single, it was so, so hard, especially when Ruth and Marvin and your parents started having children. I know you can relate to that."

Amy nodded. "You always seem so happy. So…fulfilled."

"I am. Now. It took a long time, but God and I have worked through the guilt. I've given Him all my regrets, and I'm continually learning to be present in the moment wherever I am and grateful for the life I have."

Amy dabbed her eyes with a tissue. "Thank you for sharing that. I will take it to heart."

Aunt Abigail pulled her into a bear hug. "I know you will, sweetie, I know you will."

Amy set the empty scalloped potato dish in the sink to soak then wiped off the counter. Dishes were done, and Aunt Ruth and Tracy had joined the men, watching as they took the rest of their finds out of the mesh bags and arranged them on the table.

Just before they'd sat down to dinner, one of the other Pop's Place board members had answered Whitney's group text with HAPPY TO!

Crisis averted. Without her help.

She poured herself a cup of coffee and walked to the study. The fire was still lit, creating an inviting place to think and pray.

Standing in front of the fireplace, she closed her eyes, letting her heart unload the way Aunt Abigail had done, giving God all of her regrets. Several minutes into her prayer, she heard her name, spoken in the soft, rich voice that felt like a cozy security blanket.

Miles stood in the doorway. "I wondered where you went. You were so quiet during dinner. What's going on?"

She motioned him in and then sat on the love seat. Miles took the chair that sat at an angle next to it. He folded his hands, elbows propped on his knees, leaning toward her in the listening position that had always made her feel like she was the only person in his universe.

This man... This very, very patient man.

She'd left home when she and Miles were eighteen because she'd put adventure and the lure of life outside of Canton ahead of her feelings for him. And now, all these years later, she was putting earning money for a vacation and involvement in causes that made her feel needed ahead of him. *Lord, help! Why am I doing this?* She opened her mouth but couldn't form a single word.

When he reached out and took both of her hands in his, she braced herself for another "Your plate's too full" talk. But the look on his face said it was more serious than that. Had he had it with her? She'd done her best to be present in the moment yesterday, but this man could see through her. Was he tired of trying to carry on a relationship with a woman who was only half there much of the time? Was he going to end it, right here, right now? What would that do to the kids? She couldn't let their children suffer because of her mistakes, but how could she manage to still arrange play dates with him? How could she stop at his house to pick up Colton and Natalie and look him in the eye? Those deep brown eyes that always made her feel safe and cherished and…

"…but I'm a fixer and I see how frazzled you are and what it's doing to your relationship with your kids, and it makes me want to do something. I'm sorry if I overstepped by planning our getaway yesterday, but I just wanted to—" Her fingertip over his lips ended his apology.

Amy grabbed a tissue from the box and wiped her eyes. "I want your help. I *need* your help. I have to figure out why I can't say no and why I've let this vacation with the kids take on such monumental proportions. I'm sorry I've been so distracted. You and our kids are all that's really important, so why did I let myself get so overcommitted and…." Her shoulders shook as a wave of tears started again.

Miles moved to sit beside her, wrapping his strong arms around her. She buried her face in his chest. "I'm scared you'll give up on me before I untangle myself from all of these obligations."

A low laugh rumbled in his chest. "Never." He pulled back and lifted her chin with his fingers. "I'm right here. Not going anywhere. Like I said, I'm a fixer, so I'm taking on a new project. Tell me to ease up when I overstep, but from now on you have your very own personal untangler. Let's start by joining the others and seeing if we can untangle this boat mystery. Together."

She stood and leaned into him. "That's a good place to start."

He lifted her chin again. "So is this." He bent close. His lips were about to touch hers, when her phone, silenced but not off, buzzed in her sweater pocket, interrupting the beautiful moment.

Not pulling her gaze away from his, she slipped her hand in her pocket and pushed the button on the side to decline the call. "Now, where were—" Her phone buzzed again.

"It might be important," Miles said, his breath tickling her cheek.

With a frustrated sigh, she took it out. "It's Maura Childs."

"You should take it."

Amy tapped the screen and then raised the phone to her ear. "Hi, Maura."

"Hello, Amy. I hope I'm not interrupting your family dinner, but I've found something in the archives that I think you'll want to see."

Chapter Fifteen

"When you live alone and you're as old as dirt, digging through a musty old storeroom on a Sunday afternoon is far more appealing than watching old black-and-white movies you've seen a million times." Maura stood in front of a third-floor door in the oldest building on campus. On the frosted glass window in the door, black letters, peeling in spots, spelled out ARCHIVES. The transom above the door hinted at a time long before central air-conditioning. The entire floor, now used only for storage, smelled like dust and old books.

Maura turned a white porcelain doorknob. Below it was an old-fashioned keyhole. Standing next to Miles, behind Maura, Amy pulled Violet's key out of her pocket, held it up so he could see it, and they both shook their heads. Much too small. "I get the appeal," Amy said. "We spend lots of Sunday afternoons in my grandmother's attic."

"You've found some great treasures there, haven't you?" The door creaked as Maura swung it open. "Since we met the other day, I couldn't stop thinking about Violet and the things I saw, or thought I saw, back then. Though my memory isn't what it once was, I remembered helping box up the things from Professor Conway's office after he died, and it got me wondering what happened to all of his old files and the things we took out of his desk. I assumed we would have given them to Violet, but then I remembered that the secretary and I were talking about the birthday I'd just had while we packed boxes." She snapped on a floor lamp and turned to face them. "My birthday is in August."

It took Amy a moment to understand the significance. "Professor Conway died in April."

"Yes. Violet could have come in at any time and cleaned out his things, but she didn't, and there was no need for it to be done until the fall term started."

"And by then Violet had disappeared."

Maura nodded. "So I got to thinking that we must have just stored everything up here, assuming she'd be back to claim it all at some point. Or, I should say, hoping she would."

Amy surveyed the space that reminded her very much of her grandparents' attic. Two walls were lined with file cabinets. Several old, ornate tables were laden with stacks of books. Most of the floor space was piled with labeled cardboard boxes and wooden crates, some dating back to the late eighteen hundreds. The history lover in Amy wanted to dig through every one, starting with the oldest. "All of Professor Conway's things are still here?"

"I've only found this one box." Maura led the way through the maze to a dusty box sitting open on an even dustier desk. "I'm pretty sure there's more. Anyway, what I found might just be the most exciting clue." She glanced up at them with a twinkle in her eye and then pulled out a yellowed file folder. When she opened it, Miles and Amy gasped in unison.

A treasure map.

They stared at the piece of typewriter paper with the penciled-in words and outlined shapes of islands.

"This must be a copy he made of the original," Maura said. "You said you talked to some people who saw it up close?"

"Yes. My aunt and I spoke to a couple who knew Violet well. They thought it was drawn on deer skin, probably with ink made from black walnuts."

"Hmm. My." Maura slid her glasses back up to the bridge of her nose. "Could be from the 1700s. Maybe older. Where is it now?"

"We have no idea. My guess is that Violet took it when she left. Or her abductor took it when he took her."

"Such an awful thought. Isn't it possible that she and her fiancé just went out in search of the treasure and…" Maura shook her head. "And something happened."

"We have considered that. She may have left willingly, but my aunts don't think she was the kind of person to take the boat without permission. My grandfather had let Violet and some friends take it out in the past. There was no reason for her to sneak out during the night." When Maura appeared lost in thought, Amy said, "Were there any other possible clues in the box?"

"You're welcome to look. It appears to me it's just class notes. And some old tea bags. I wish I could give you free rein to dig through all of these boxes, but there are rules. I'll start over by the door and do a clockwise sweep." She smiled up at Miles. "I'll yell if I need some muscle."

Maura walked toward the door. She was so short that, within seconds, Amy could only see the top of her head bobbing behind towers of boxes. "She was flirting with you," Amy whispered.

Miles laughed. "I'm used to it. I melt the hearts of all my elderly patients."

"Bet you've left a trail of broken hearts." Amy nudged her shoulder against his arm. "A trail of *old* broken hearts."

His dark eyes crinkled at the corners. "I have been known to make a few younger women weak in the knees."

Amy grinned then pretended to swoon, knowing he'd catch her. He did.

"We have to get to work, woman," Miles whispered into her hair. When he pulled back, clearly reluctantly, he pointed at the box.

"You take this pile." Amy lifted half a dozen file folders from the box and held them out to him. "I'll take the rest."

They found two wobbly desk chairs, each with a missing caster wheel, and rolled them, *clunk-clunk-clunk*, up to the desk. After fifteen minutes of searching through notes on Renaissance artists, Amy was about to give up. But the next paper, the first in a paper-clipped stack, was titled *Sea Dog Sam, Pirate of the Upper Mississippi*. She grabbed Miles by the arm and showed it to him.

> *Sea Dog Sam was a grizzled old man by the time I met him in 1930. Bowed and bent, he leaned on a walking stick made from the root of a hawthorn tree. Under that tree, somewhere on an island in the Mississippi, he had buried the cache he'd found under a bridge near what is now called*

Harrison Lake. I will do my best to tell his story the way Sea Dog told it to me.
William J. Conway

The next page was titled "The Story of Sea Dog Sam." Amy held it where Miles could read along with her.

'Twas the summer of 1854. I was but a lad of ten and two, or maybe three. Truth is, I never did know when I was born due to the fact that my mother up and died when I came into the world and my father left me in the care of his spinster sister, who knew very little about the care of children. That was to my advantage since, much like in the yarns spun by my dear departed friend and mentor Samuel Langhorne Clemens, her discombobulation allowed me to run wild and free and be the child the Almighty intended all children to be. So it was that on a blistering hot day in July I was walking barefoot along the riverbank in search of gem rocks to sell to Mr. Pickens who sold gewgaws in his general store, when I came upon a group of men huddled around a fire. These were not men familiar to me, and I soon realized they were up to no good. But it was a kind of no good that called to the heart of a young lad like me, for betwixt them was spread a piece of hide on which a large man with fingers the size of fat sausages was drawing a map. After a bit he jabbed at the map and said, "Here, boys. Here we will find Blackbeard's treasure."

Amy looked up into Miles's wide eyes. "Is this fact or fiction?"

Miles shrugged. "No clue. Weren't river pirates long gone by 1854?"

"I would have thought so. William Conway was a history professor. Is this fact, or was he trying his hand at becoming a novelist? Aunt Ruth said Violet used to make up bedtime stories for them that mixed fact and fiction. Maybe that's something she learned from her father."

"Could be. I guess we need to read the whole thing and then do some research." Miles nodded toward the stacks of boxes hiding Maura's small frame. "Do you think she'll let us take it?" he asked.

"Maybe we can copy it. And the map. Or at least take pictures. And then I think you and I should…" Amy shook her head. "No. It's a crazy thought."

The dimple on his cheek that only showed when he smiled wide made an appearance. "Pretty sure it's the same thing I'm thinking."

"What do you think I'm thinking?"

"That we both have Wednesday off."

When the final bell rang on Monday afternoon, Amy let out a sigh of relief. The day that started at five in the morning by cleaning for Niesha's bridal shower had dragged. She'd struggled all day to stay present in the moment, her thoughts constantly wandering to an X on a treasure map.

During her lunch break, Miles had sent a text telling her he'd talked to someone from the Illinois Department of Natural Resources and had already submitted a metal detecting permit for Teal Island. Instead of grading papers during the rest of her break, she'd made a list of things they'd need. Jeff had said she could borrow his metal detector, shovel, headphones, pointer, and a "finds" pouch. Last night, when she couldn't quiet her mind to get to sleep, she'd watched several training videos he'd recommended, adding terms like ground balancing, discrimination, gain, and sensitivity to her new detectorist vocabulary.

She'd need the hiking boots she hadn't worn in two years and a pair of work gloves. She'd pack sandwiches and a thermos of decaf to warm them. Miles was bringing his own metal detecting gear, headlamps, and a machete for clearing the underbrush. And she'd need the Sea Dog Sam book manuscript Maura said she would copy and get to her before Wednesday.

After her room emptied, she took out her phone. The first five lists in her notes app seemed to taunt her, as if saying "How can you even think of hunting for treasure with all of *this*?" She ran through the checklist for her Cyber Monday Etsy site launch. Only three things yet to finish. Everything looked good for tonight's shower. They'd kept it simple, and for once, she'd delegated. All she had to do was serve tea and coffee.

At the beginning of the school year, she'd scheduled a personal day for Wednesday, November 22, intending to use it for pie baking and any other help Tracy needed getting ready for Thanksgiving dinner. When she'd told Miles about it several weeks ago, he'd rearranged his schedule to help her "because I need to learn how to bake a pie." She hadn't fallen for the excuse at the time, but it had been a fortuitous move. Now they'd be spending the day before Thanksgiving hunting for buried treasure.

She swiped to her calendar, and a sick, cold dread clutched her middle. Thursday. Thanksgiving. She'd wanted to surprise Matt and Jana with a National Adoption Day banner, even though the day was already past. And gifts. Six weeks ago, before she became the girl who couldn't say no to anything, she'd designed matching shirts for them. Jana's would say "Wanted. Chosen. Loved. Adopted." in pink and purple letters. Matt's would be subtler. Slate gray with black lettering. "Official Member of the Allen Clan." But she'd never ordered them. Was it too late? And what about gifts? Something special, to make their eyes light up.

There was only one thing she was sure would do that. One thing that would make up for every "too busy" moment in this last month.

Jana and Natalie came in, holding hands. "Can we get popcorn on our way home?" Jana asked. "And can Natalie come home with us so we can get dressed for the shower together? She can wear my…"

Three days. Could she pull it all together? Maybe Miles would help. Miles. What would her gift to her kids do to his kids? Was this all a mistake? Was it worth it? Would she regret this when all the work landed on her? And was she becoming one of those moms who plied her children with guilt gifts? No, she was simply giving her kids something she'd always known she'd give in to someday. Wasn't she?

"Mooom!" Jana's impatient but laughing voice broke through her scattered thoughts. Jana turned to Natalie.

Natalie joined in the laughter. "My dad does that too. I think they're thinking about"—she shielded her mouth with her hand—"each other!" With that, the two dissolved into giggles.

"What's going on in here?" Sara walked in, coat and purse over her arm. Her question only brought another round of seven-year-old silliness. Amy sent the girls to the reading corner and reminded them to "use your inside voices."

"You're packed up early," Amy said. "And by that I mean you're leaving on time." She winked at Sara, who reminded Amy so much of herself in her early years of teaching, often putting in extra time. Sara's passion for her students showed in everything she did.

"I have a couple of finishing touches to add to the suncatcher." How Sara found time to be creative, Amy couldn't fathom. Though it probably helped to have an amazingly supportive husband. Amy had seen in-progress pictures of the piece she was making for Pop's Place. "I still need to apply the patina solution and polish it."

"I can't wait to see it. After I get my Etsy store up and running, I want to get back to some just-for-fun creativity." Designing templates and worksheets to sell had required some level of creativity, but the rush to get them ready had stolen a lot of the enjoyment.

"How's your balancing act coming along?" Sara asked. "I gather Mom has been nagging you about being too busy."

Amy nodded. "It's part of the big sister job description. I hope she knows that, even if I act annoyed sometimes, I appreciate her concern. And yours. I've learned some painful lessons in the past couple of weeks. I was always busy before kids. It gave me a sense of purpose, of identity. I'm learning to make the right priorities and remember my true purpose. Anyway, one more week. Eight days, and I'll be free as a bird."

"When you get your wings back, let's schedule a spa date to celebrate your freedom. I'm feeling due for a mommy break too, and who better to spend it with than my aunt Amy?"

"Sounds heavenly." Amy hugged her. "Thinking about a massage and facial will help me through the next few days. Thank you. See you tonight."

As Amy turned her attention back to the girls, her phone buzzed with a call from Aunt Abigail.

"Hi. Everything okay?"

A hearty laugh echoed through the phone. "Yes. Didn't mean to scare you. I guess I haven't talked to you on the phone for a long time. Anyway, Ruth and I are at the house, looking through things in the attic, and I found something. Some *things*. Not going to tell you anything more than that until you get here."

Glancing at the clock, Amy suppressed a sigh. Why now, when she had so much to do before Niesha's shower? But what if Aunt Abigail had found something that would solve the Violet mystery? "We'll be right…"

Matt running into the room stopped her words. "Mom, come quick. Lucas Cartwright…he's hurt."

Chapter Sixteen

"In the gym." Matt panted. "Hurry."

Amy grabbed her phone. "Girls, run and get Principal Walker and tell her to come to the gym. Then you two stay in the office."

Matt was already running down the hall. As she ran behind him, she tried to keep her thoughts from manufacturing scenarios. Nothing could make her believe Matt had started a fight. She could imagine him defending himself, maybe even striking back if provoked, but Lucas was twice his size. "What…happened?" She was out of breath by the time she caught up with him in front of the doors to the gym.

Matt yanked open one of the doors. He ran into the gym and pointed to a spot under the bleachers.

Far back in the shadows, Lucas sat, knees pulled up to his chest. Amy's first reaction was relief that he wasn't lying there unconscious. She dropped to her knees and crawled to him. "Lucas. It's Miss Allen. Tell me where you're hurt."

In the little light that filtered through the bench seats, Amy could see tear tracks shining on his freckled face. His left arm was propped on top of his knees. "My arm. He twisted it. I think it's broken."

Amy looked back at Matt, crouched by the opening. Before she could question him again, she heard running footsteps.

Kelly Walker crawled in beside them on hands and knees. Together, they gently prodded Lucas's arm. "We need to call your parents and get you in for X-rays," Kelly said.

"D-don't call my dad. My m-mom's at work, but she can probably get off early."

"If his mother is okay with it, I can take him to urgent care," Amy said.

Kelly rested a hand on Lucas's shoe. "I'll go call her. Can you scoot out of here using your good arm?"

"I th-think so."

Matt stripped off his sweatshirt and crawled next to Lucas. "We should make a sling."

"Good idea." A swell of pride filled Amy as she took the sweatshirt and carefully slid it under Lucas's injured arm, giving it support, and tied the cuffs behind his neck.

"I'll take your backpack," Matt said.

"Thanks."

Amy studied Lucas's expression. Nothing, except maybe genuine gratitude. What had happened between these two?

Lucas inched out on his bottom, grimacing with every move. When he was free of the bleachers, Amy helped him ease onto a bench. "We'll wait here until Mrs. Walker comes back. Matt, can you go get the girls, and all of you get your jackets on and get my purse and coat and meet us here?"

"Okay." Matt took off running.

"I'm sorry this happened." She had no idea if she was apologizing for her son or maybe just saying she was sorry Lucas had gotten hurt. Could he have been fooling around on the bleachers and simply fallen?"

"Thanks. Those guys are creeps."

Guys. Plural. Matt and Colton? No. Not possible. "Can you tell me what happened?"

"I was waiting for the bus and Brody Stahl—he's in eighth grade—showed up with another guy. They pushed me behind the building and then they started shoving me around. When I tried to run, Brody grabbed my arm and started twisting it. I thought he was going to pull it off. Then Matt showed up out of nowhere and started screaming for them to leave me alone or he was going to call the cops." Lucas smiled for the first time. "You shoulda seen them run."

Another rush of pride. And a huge sigh of relief.

Kelly hurried into the gym. "Mrs. Cartwright will meet you at urgent care. She told me to thank you profusely. Your kids are on their way." She sat next to Lucas. "Tell me what happened."

As they talked, Amy texted Aunt Abigail and told her she'd be late.

Matt, Jana, and Natalie ran in, all breathless. Matt held out her keys and then pulled them back. "I'll drive."

Though his comedic timing might be off, it was clear his entire countenance had changed. Amy took the keys and gave him a quick hug. "Lucas told me what you did. I'm so proud of you."

"It was nothing. I was just heaping coals of burning fire on his head."

Amy smiled at him. "That's not nothing, Matt. That's a very big something."

As they walked to the car, she overheard Lucas talking to Matt. "Thanks again. And sorry about your camera. I was kind of a jerk. I'll bring it back. I figure you're gonna need it, 'cause when my arm heals I'm gonna challenge you to another hoops contest, and somebody has to record my win."

Matt laughed, a sound that was music to Amy's ears. "Bring it on, big guy."

Aunt Abigail knelt on the floor with an old pillow as a cushion. Aunt Ruth perched on a low stool beside her. A large green plastic bin sat on the floor between them. A shiny pink box with a black lid sat on top of the bin. Aunt Abigail's arm rested on the box.

Amy pointed to the corner with the beanbag chair and a pile of faded patio chair pillows that matched the one Aunt Abigail knelt on, and told the kids to sit there to eat the caramel corn they'd picked up at Popelstopp's Popcorn Shop. Then she turned her attention to the pink box. It had to be the one Aunt Abigail had seen Grandma Pearl open. The one that had made her gasp. "Is something going to jump out?" Amy asked, kneeling next to Aunt Abigail.

"Maybe." Aunt Abigail smiled like the Cheshire cat. "Robin and Tracy are on their way home."

Home. It dawned on Amy that Aunt Abigail had said, "I'm at *the* house." Not Tracy's house. In her mind, this was still home. What ever was in the box, she was glad Aunt Abigail had found it. It had to be hard to live so far away and hear from her sister about all of the treasures they'd uncovered since Grandma Pearl died.

Laughter rang in the room below the stairs. Robin stepped into the attic first, with Tracy right behind her. "What's in the box?" Tracy asked, not bothering with greetings. She and Robin knelt on the floor.

The aunts exchanged a look of shared sadness. "Let's start with the happy thing," Aunt Abigail said. She set the shoebox aside and put her hands on top of the green bin. "Drum roll, please." Aunt Abigail broadened her secretive smile and waited while the other four tapped a rumbling beat on the plank floor with their feet.

With painful slowness, Aunt Abigail lifted the plastic lid. White tissue paper covered the contents. Aunt Ruth reached down and lifted one layer. Aunt Abigail lifted the next, and a collective gasp filled the room.

"Is that..." Amy reached out and touched a single pearl button. As Aunt Abigail grasped the fabric and stood, bits and pieces of the description Amy had read in Violet's bride book came back to her. Romantic design. Sheer lace bodice. Sabrina-style neckline. Long, sheer, pointed sleeves that snapped at the wrists.

"The wedding dress." Jana stood at Amy's side, her hushed voice filled with wonder.

"Ohhh..." Natalie, next to Jana, used the same tone.

Aunt Ruth picked up the full skirt in both arms so it wouldn't touch the floor. Tiered lace cascaded in elegant ripples, a bit of satin tulle peeking out at the bottom.

"There's another dress!" Jana pointed to the bottom of the bin.

"Actually, there are two," Aunt Ruth said. "Two little white dresses. These were made by Violet for Aunt Abigail and me. We were going to be her flower girls. Though we were a bit younger than you and Natalie, Aunt Abigail and I are pretty good at sewing, and I think that, with a few adjustments, we can make them fit the two of you just perfectly." She gestured for Jana to take them out.

"Could we wear them to Niesha's wedding, Mom?" Jana lifted one of the white lace dresses as if it might disintegrate in her hands and handed it carefully to Natalie then lifted the next one. When she looked at Amy, her eyes sparkled. "These are the prettiest, prettiest dresses I have ever, ever seen in my whole life." She pointed at the wedding gown. "Can Niesha wear that one?"

"I think that's a great idea, if she wants to wear it." Amy felt the prickle of tears behind her eyes. What a beautiful sense of closure. Two young women, both left on their own too young, both finding a sense of belonging with the Allens. They may never learn what happened to Violet, but Niesha would be able to fulfill her dream.

They folded the dress and put it back in the bin. "I'll take it in to have it cleaned tomorrow," Aunt Ruth said.

"Maybe...," Amy said, the picture forming in her head. "We should give it to her—"

"Tonight?" Aunt Ruth and Aunt Abigail spoke together, both voices barely containing a squeal of anticipation.

"I can't wait to see her face," Tracy said. She pointed to the shoebox. "That one has something bad in it?"

"The things aren't bad," Aunt Ruth answered. "In fact, we were thrilled to find them. It's what they represent that's bad."

"Enough with the dramatics, Mom." Robin picked up the shoebox, shook it gently, and then handed it to Aunt Abigail. "You two do love to torture people."

"Years of practice," Aunt Abigail said. "Did I ever tell you about the time we hid all of your uncle Noah's Christmas presents? He woke up on Christmas morning and there was a big pile for me and a big pile for Ruthy and not a single thing for him except a lump of coal with his name on it."

"He must have been six at the time," Aunt Ruth said. "I don't think I'd ever heard him howl like he did that morning. And then Dad stepped in and, to punish us, made us bring them all out and sit and watch him open them. We didn't get to touch our gifts until after Christmas dinner. It was—"

"Mother." Robin pointed to the box. "Enough." Her stern face made them all laugh.

"Okay. Here we go." Aunt Abigail tipped the box up to show the top. Addressed to Pearl Allen, two rows of stamps, no return address. Curled shreds of old tape still clung to the top and sides. Amy scooted closer to read the postmark.

Crystal City, Missouri

August 17, 1955

"That's exactly two months after Violet went missing," Amy said.

Aunt Ruth nodded. "That's what caught our attention first."

Aunt Abigail's fingers curled around the lift-off top, but she didn't open it. "I don't have a lot of memories of *River Dancer*, but I do remember Ruthy and I sobbing when we found out it was gone. Not so much because of the boat, but because of what we'd left on board." Slowly, she lifted the lid then angled the box to show its contents.

Two dolls nestled side by side. Aunt Ruth reached for the dark-haired doll in a plaid dress with a white collar. "I begged and begged for a Betsy McCall doll. I couldn't believe it when Violet gave it to me for helping at her estate sale. I'd left her on the boat on purpose because we'd invited friends to go out on the river with us the next night."

"Me too." Aunt Abigail picked up the other one, a baby doll with painted-on hair. The eyes fluttered open with a soft click when she held it upright. "Meet Tiny Tears. I called her Penny." She fingered the white nightgown trimmed in pink as if she were a little girl again.

"Wait." Tracy's mouth puckered like it often did when she was trying to solve a problem. "Someone sent these back two months after the boat disappeared, but Grandma Pearl never gave them to you?" Her expression reflected the confusion Amy felt.

Aunt Abigail shook her head. "Mom never mentioned them. Very strange, because she knew we were upset about losing them."

"She took us shopping to replace them," Aunt Ruth said, "but I remember crying in the store and saying you can't replace someone you love. Now I wonder if I was really thinking about Violet."

Aunt Abigail reached into the box and pulled out a folded piece of paper. "This might explain why Mom was afraid to give them to us." She opened the paper and read the single line. "'Your silence is greatly appreciated.'"

"What in the world?" Robin took the paper. "No signature. Who...?" The question floated in the room, unanswerable. At least for now.

June 19, 1955

I have always respected Violet's privacy. She is an adult, and, under normal circumstances, I would never look at her personal things. These are not normal circumstances, so I am sitting in her room after everyone else is asleep, reading her diary.

She records funny things my children say and writes such kind things about Howard and me that it breaks my heart a little more with every word. Her descriptions of tender moments with Lenny are so precious. I'm touched by her honesty as they strive together to keep their vow of purity. Unbeknownst to me, they often include Ruth, Abigail, and sometimes even Noah on picnics and outings to act as chaperones. Her love for God flows like a silver thread, woven into every page.

Vi wrote about finding the treasure map and showing it to Professor Janvier. She was so excited that he thought it could be at least a hundred years old, maybe more. Then there are a couple of entries about wedding plans and a movie date with Lenny. All seemed normal until June 16, the night she disappeared. She wrote:

Don called a few minutes ago. He said some very dangerous people know about the treasure map. He told me to leave the house right away. Then he hung up. I don't know what to do. If I leave, they may hurt the people I love. If I cooperate and give them the map, will that be the end of it? Will they leave us alone? Who are they, and how did they hear about the map? Only eight people know about it. Six of us made a pact, and I know Professor Janvier, Pearl, and Lenny would never tell anyone, so it had to be one of the other four. I want so badly to give in to anger, but the verses in Romans 12 Pearl and I are memorizing together keep coming back to me. "Bless them which persecute you: bless, and curse not," and "avenge not yourselves, but rather give place unto wrath: for it is written, Vengeance is mine; I will repay, saith the Lord." I just hope God's vengeance comes before it is too late for me. In the meantime, I have devised a bit of trickery.

That was her last entry. Now I remember hearing the phone ring late that night. Violet was still up, and she answered it. Why, oh why, didn't I get out of bed to check on her, to ask her who had called?

There will be no sleep tonight. In the morning, I will show this to the police.

Chapter Seventeen

The tears on Niesha's face were happy ones. Amy and Tracy engulfed her in a hug as she said, "N-nobody ever…" She didn't need to finish. Growing up in the foster system, bouncing from home to home and town to town, she'd never experienced what she now had—a family comprised of college, church, and work friends, the moms from Pop's Place, and all the Allen family women.

After two silly games, Carrie Ellis brought out the most stunning cupcakes Amy had ever seen. Incredibly, she'd chosen to decorate them with lace and pearls, as if they'd been designed to match the dress that sat in a box wrapped in silver paper and a massive white bow.

Lisa, the maid of honor, sat on Niesha's right as she opened gifts, handing wrapping paper and bags to Robin and creating a paper plate bouquet of bows for the bride to carry at the rehearsal. Amy sat on her left, making a list of gifts and givers. Niesha's colors for their St. Louis apartment were denim blue and bright yellow.

As the pile of sheets, towels, serving dishes, and kitchen utensils grew, Niesha seemed once again on the verge of happy tears. After opening the last one sitting on the coffee table in front of her, her exuberant mood sobered. "'Thank you' doesn't begin to cover what I'm feeling right now. If someone had asked me a year ago what my wedding would be like, I would have said it would just be two people standing in front of a judge at the courthouse. I never let myself imagine what it would be like to have this much support."

Amy looked at Aunt Abigail and gave a slight nod. Tracy crouched with her camera a few feet from Niesha as Aunt Abigail stood, reached behind her chair, and took out the box that was eight inches high and almost three feet long. "One last gift," she said as she walked across the room and set the box on Niesha's lap.

"It's huge," Niesha said. She pulled off the bow and handed it to Lisa then carefully slid her finger beneath each piece of tape and handed off the white paper. The room was silent as she opened the box. And then she gasped. "Is this…Violet's dress?"

Aunt Abigail nodded. Lisa reached for the box as Niesha grasped the gown by the shoulders and stood, holding it out at arm's length as the scalloped skirt unfolded. "It's… It's… Gorgeous. Where did you find it?"

The aunts told the story of hours in Grandma's attic searching for anything that would lead them to clues about Violet's disappearance. By now, everyone in the circle had heard about the "River Dan" name board and the things they'd found in the river. The one thing Amy hadn't shared with anyone outside the family was the sketch of the treasure map she and Miles had found in the college's archives. That they would keep secret until after Wednesday.

Amy had taken the full-length mirror off her bathroom door and hidden it behind the couch. Now she got up and held it in front of Niesha. With Lisa's help, Niesha turned the dress around, clasping it to her chest. Her dark ringlets cascaded over the lace bodice.

"I remember that dress." Oriana Beecher sat next to Brooke. She hadn't said a word since arriving. Now, her small voice seemed tinged with confusion. As she lifted the scalloped hem to examine the intricate stitches, her eyes widened. "I helped Violet make it. We all did."

"All?" Aunt Ruth's voice echoed Aunt Abigail's.

"You were part of that?" Aunt Ruth asked.

"Oh yes. I was quite the seamstress in my day. We spent hours sewing on those pearls."

"Who else helped?" Amy asked.

"Pearl, of course. And Connie Sherman."

"Sherman?" That name rang a bell for Amy. *Leonard Sherman.* "Who was she?"

"Lenny Therwood's grandmother." Oriana seemed confused that everyone wouldn't know that.

Amy's brain scrambled to make sense of what she'd just learned. Lenny's grandmother's last name was Sherman. Could Lenny have taken her name? She thought back to what she remembered of the obituary. Leonard Sherman had died in his eighties. In Rockport, Illinois. His wife was named Violet. They had a daughter named Abby Ruth. Too many coincidences to be coincidences. She hadn't searched for an obituary for Violet Sherman. Was she Violet Conway?

Was she still alive?

Would they be putting her, or anyone else, at risk by trying to contact her?

Just after eight thirty, the last gift was carried to Niesha's car and Amy hugged her and Lisa goodbye. Miles had picked up Natalie and dropped off Matt, and Amy had given him a rushed and whispered account of what Oriana had said. Only the Allen women were left in the house. Amy hugged the kids and sent them up to bed then called a halt to the cleanup. "Everybody grab a cup of tea and join me at the table." She opened her laptop and found Leonard Sherman's obituary. She hadn't mentioned it to anyone when she'd found it, assuming it was just too far-fetched to be a lead. Now she turned the screen so the four women settling into seats with mugs of tea could read it.

One by one, lips parted. Aunt Ruth was the first to find her voice. "Leonard Sherman. Violet. Violet C. Sherman. Could the C be for Conway? And Abby Ruth." She shook her head slowly. "It *has* to be."

"How far is Rockport?" Aunt Abigail asked.

"About an hour south of here," Tracy answered.

Amy tapped *Abby Ruth Matson* on her phone. "Look!" A few more taps brought her to a social media account. Without thinking twice, Amy sent her a friend request. In moments, it was accepted. "I'm going to message her." But before she finished typing, a message popped up.

> Hi Amy. Thank you for the friend request. I think I know why you're reaching out to me. Would you be available for a phone call? I'll be up until about eleven tonight, or anytime tomorrow. If you call in the next hour, I will be with my mother.

"Her…mother." Aunt Ruth said the words over Aunt Abigail's sharp inhale.

Violet was alive.

The next message was a phone number.

Amy slid the phone across the table, leaving it between Aunt Abigail's right hand and Aunt Ruth's left. "You two should talk to her first."

Aunt Ruth's finger trembled slightly as she made the call then tapped the speaker icon.

"Hello. This is Abby Ruth."

Aunt Ruth smiled. "And this is..." She nodded at her sister.

"Abby."

"And Ruth."

"My girls!" The second voice was clearer and stronger than Amy would have expected for a woman in her late eighties.

"Violet." Once again the aunts spoke at the same time, neither seeming to know what to say next.

"Oh, how I've missed you girls. And your darling brother. I was devastated when I read that he'd passed. It was so hard, not being there when you went through so many losses. When I read Pearl's obituary..." Her voice cracked. "I'm so grateful you had her for such a long time. Did she tell you everything?"

"She didn't tell us anything," Aunt Abigail said. "We just found the box with our dolls in it."

"Dolls? You got your dolls back?"

"They were sent two months after you...left. Did you send them?"

"No. They were still on the boat. I tried to grab them." The distress in her voice was evident. And escalating. "I stuffed them in my purse. Just before Don made me...jump."

When Violet began breathing much too fast, interspersed with short sobs, Tracy held up her hand. "She's having a panic attack," she whispered under her breath. "Abby Ruth, would it be possible for us all to meet in person?" Tracy looked at Amy. It was clear an idea was taking shape in her mind. "Do you have plans for Thanksgiving?"

"Yes. My son and his family will be here."

"This is Tracy, Noah's oldest. How about the day after? We always make too much food. My husband and I are living in Grandma Pearl's house. Would you be able to join us here for lunch on Friday?"

"That would…" Violet paused, likely seeking an okay from her daughter. "That would be wonderful. I would love to see the house again. And Canton. So many memories. But it's okay now. The danger is over, and we can be together again." She let out a long sigh. "May I bring a pan of apple buckle?"

"Yes, please!" Aunt Ruth's eyes, shimmering with tears, lit up. "I remember making it with you. I have your recipe, but it never turns out quite like yours."

Violet laughed. "Every good cook leaves something out when she shares a recipe. I will tell you that little secret, and everything else, when I see you on Friday."

Jana was in one of her nonstop talking moods on Tuesday afternoon as they got ready for the fashion show—likely brought on by her adorable costume and the chance to wear a touch of blush and lipstick for her onstage performance. Now, as they drove into town, she yelled, "Look, Mom!" from the back seat. "A dog just like Scrappy in the movie. Over there, by the flower store."

Amy glanced to her right. A black, white, and brown terrier sat by the door of the florist shop, probably waiting for its owner. "He's cute."

"So you *do* want a dog. Did you hear that, Matt? Mom wants a dog. We should get a boy dog so we can name him Scrappy. Isn't that the cutest name? Matt? Mom, he's being crabby again."

Amy wasn't surprised. Yesterday had ended on a high note. Matt was still awake when everyone had left the shower, and Amy finally got the chance to hear the whole story. Matt had spent the day trying to work up the courage to talk to Lucas. When the bell rang at the end of the day, he'd rushed outside, hoping to catch him standing in the bus line. That way, there would be people around and Lucas would have to leave right after Matt asked him, as nicely as he could, to please give back the camera. But as Matt had approached, two big kids he recognized as friends of Kai forced Lucas to walk with them behind the school. "They didn't do anything until the last bus left. When they started hurting Lucas, I didn't even stop to think, Mom, I just started yelling."

Amy had hugged him and told him again how proud she was. This morning he'd been all smiles, but Lucas had stayed home, so he didn't get his camera back, and now he was afraid Kai might have heard a distorted story from his friends. "What if he thinks I'm the one who picked a fight?" he'd said before they got into the car. She'd answered, "Don't worry. Kai knows you."

"Everybody has bad days, Jana," she said over her shoulder, and then she glanced at Matt in the rearview mirror. "Do you want me to talk to Kai? Or be with you when you do?" She was doing the hovering mom thing, but she wanted him to know he didn't have to do this alone.

"No. I got it." He sounded like a man sentenced to walk the plank.

She parked behind Pearls of Wisdom and aimed a smile toward the back seat before she handed Matt her vacation notebook. "Talk to Kai about vacation. I called Golden Sky, and they aren't fully booked the week we're going. Robin loves the idea, so if you can get Kai excited about a dude ranch, they'll go with us. Might be more fun with another kid along, right?"

"Can Colton come with us instead? Please?"

"And Natalie? I don't want to go alone. And I don't want to learn to ride a horse all by myself. And I bet you want Dr. Miles to go too." Jana giggled.

This was getting ridiculous. "You won't be alone, and…" Amy let it drop.

"Can't I just stay home tonight?" Matt's voice was back to whine mode. "A bunch of kids in my class get to stay home alone."

"One more year. For now, you do have the choice of either staying at Colton's or coming to the fundraiser." She winked in the rearview mirror, trying to lighten his mood. "You'll love the fashion show."

A giggle came from the other side of the back seat. "He could be in the show! What costume should we make him wear?"

"We could always have two models with bell sleeves. I've got lots of jingle bells in my classroom. We could—"

"Funny. Seriously, Mom, I looked it up. Missouri doesn't have any laws about what age a kid can be left alone. It's okay as long as the parent thinks the kid is mature enough to stay safe and not do dumb stuff and you provide for my basic needs. Like stuffed pretzels and peanut butter cakes."

She heard the smile in his voice, and her shoulders relaxed. "Not a chance." On her grocery run, she'd indulged in a few treats for herself and the kids. She'd labeled one box MOM ONLY and put it on a top shelf in the pantry with orders that they could have anything they wanted except for her chocolate cakes topped with peanut butter creme and smothered in milk chocolate. She could easily imagine a scene playing out similar to the one in the Garden of Eden—Matt questioning Jana with "Did Mom really say…?"

"Pleeeease?"

"I believe you are mature enough to take care of yourself, my son, and I know you would be careful and sensible and safe, but…I do not trust you to stay out of the pantry."

"Moooom!"

The whine wasn't serious. Amy laughed and opened the car door. "Let's go."

They were only halfway up the stairs to Terry and Robin's apartment when the door opened and Robin stood framed in the doorway. "Mom just called."

"Oh?" The look on Robin's face didn't portend anything bad. "What did she say?" Amy stepped into the apartment behind Matt. Rocket, Terry and Robin's Australian shepherd, came to greet them, tail wagging furiously as Matt bent down to scratch behind his ears.

"She had a last-minute brainstorm. She's bringing Katerina to the fundraiser, hoping it might jog some memories."

"And she's probably hoping she'll open up and talk when Silva isn't around. I'm kind of surprised he's letting her go." Amy waved at Terry and Kai, who were arranging a board game on their card table in the living room. Terry greeted them, and Kai called to Matt, "Hey! I got something for you."

Kai pulled back the chair next to him. On the seat was Matt's video camera.

"Where did you get that?" Matt took three long strides toward the table.

"I heard what happened. I used my smooth powers of persuasion to convince Brody and Evan to walk with me to Lucas's house to apologize for beating him up."

Matt's eyes widened in admiration.

"Okay, it might have been the school counselor telling them they'd be off the soccer team if they didn't go apologize that actually convinced them. I tagged along, and when Lucas found out you were my cousin, he handed over the camera and told me to give it to you. Don't let it go to your head, but he may or may not have said you were cool."

Amy took a moment to savor the grin on her son's face.

Robin grabbed her coat and the bag containing her costume then gave a couple of instructions to Terry about supper. As soon as she closed the door behind them, a question practically burst from her mouth. "What's this about you and Miles going treasure hunting...alone?"

Stopping halfway down the steps, Amy turned and rolled her eyes. "What did Tracy tell you?"

"That instead of helping her bake pies on Wednesday, you and Miles are taking his boat out to Teal Island to look for treasure. And you're packing a picnic lunch and borrowing that cute blue hat and glove set she bought last year—"

"What hat?"

"Okay, that might have been something she added. She just wants you to look fetching."

"'Fetching'? My sister actually said that? Your mother is even too young to use 'fetching.' That's a Grandma Pearl word. And besides, we're going to be tromping around on a swampy island. I need to be warm and practical, not 'fetching.'"

Robin fastened her seat belt. "She has your best interests at heart."

"I know."

"About the treasure hunt. I feel out of the loop. You found the map?"

"Sorry. I didn't leave you out on purpose. You guys left Tracy and Jeff's before we got back on Sunday, and I've just been…"

"Way too busy?"

Amy started to take offense, but Robin's understanding smile made that impossible. She told Robin about finding the pencil-drawn copy of Professor Conway's treasure map. "There's an X drawn on Teal Island. Of course, there's no way of knowing if it was put there by the person who buried the treasure, or to mark where it was found, or to throw off enemies. I doubt we'll actually find anything. We just want to go have a look around."

"Sure you don't want company? It was so fun with most of the family searching for *River Dancer*. Wouldn't you rather go with all of us?"

Amy suddenly saw how it might look. A few days ago, almost the entire family had been involved in a fun hunt for clues along the river. Now she was taking it upon herself to do this search without them. But *with* Miles. "It was fun with the whole family last week, but the temps are dropping. Thursday is going to be sunny and a high of fifty-three. Too chilly for the kids, unfortunately. Probably too cold for me." Her voice sounded strained, even to herself. "Miles wants to winterize the boat on Friday, so it's kind of our only chance and—"

Robin laughed.

"You...weren't serious."

"Not in the least. Tromping around on a swampy island is not my idea of a great date, but I bet the two of you, *alone*, will have a wonderful day." She winked.

Amy rolled her eyes. "I'm not usually this gullible. I hope my sense of humor comes back when life eases up a bit." They chatted about costumes and Amy's swampy island date until they drove into the church parking lot.

As Amy parked, another car pulled up on their left. Aunt Ruth and Katerina. Before Katerina's door opened, Aunt Ruth shot out of the driver's side and ran around the front of her car. Amy rolled the window down. "Just compliment her," Aunt Ruth whispered, grimacing. "She found it in her closet." She turned away and opened Katerina's door.

The first thing Amy saw was peep-toe red shoes and red-painted toenails. Slowly, a vision in a fur coat with padded shoulders stepped out. The coat gaped open, revealing a swath of red. With crumpled paper flames attached.

She'd kept her costume. For sixty-eight years.

"Why, Katerina," Amy exclaimed. "You look positively...fetching."

Chapter Eighteen

The Sunday school room in the church basement looked like a windstorm had ripped through a department store. Scattered clothes lay across a multi-colored rug, a plastic stove and refrigerator, a Little Tykes slide, a playhouse, and an assortment of hooks three feet from the floor. A large bowl of safety pins sat on a low table next to a roll of duct tape and three pairs of scissors. Rose Napolitano, owner of Great Lengths Salon, and two of her employees had volunteered to do hair and makeup. A haze of hairspray hung over the room.

"Just like the first time," Katerina said. She sat on a folding chair, surveying the scene like a queen. Rose had finished "touching up" the crooked lipstick and eyeshadow Katerina had applied at home. There was no time to do anything about the pedicure she'd given herself, but everyone would be understanding. At least Amy hoped they would.

"I bet that was fun." Amy stood beside her, unable to sit in her costume. "Were you a member of this church?"

"Oh no. Silva was an atheist. That was before we came to know Jesus. Did you know your grandparents led us to the Lord? Soon after Vi…" Katerina turned her head toward the door, tracking Brooke as she walked in wearing a narrow skirt with a navy jacket, both covered in rows and rows of pins. "Don's girlfriend, Ellen, wore that." She looked up at Amy. "Did she ever confront Don about his crush on Violet?"

"I...don't know." Should she leave this alone, or was it relevant? "How did you find out about it?"

"Anyone with eyes in their head could see it. He fawned all over Vi. Didn't make Lenny any too happy."

"Attention!" Whitney's voice silenced the chatter. "Guests are seated, and it's time to go on. Line up, please."

The next forty-five minutes were filled with laughter. Amy stood at the door of the side room, whispering last-minute reminders and helping to straighten costumes before the models stepped onto the platform. The boxy house dress followed the card-again, and then came the bell sleeves. The audience responded just the way she'd hoped, and it warmed her heart that the single moms who lived at Pop's Place received the loudest applause.

Amy squeezed Jana's shoulders just before it was her turn to walk across the platform. She wished she could frame the smile her daughter aimed up at her.

"And now," Whitney said, "we have one of our younger ladies sporting a stylish pinafore." Jana walked out in her dress with giant number fours pinned to the front and back. "I'm sure you'll agree this is the cutest pin-a-four you've seen in a long time." Waving at the audience, Jana stopped on the *X* taped to the floor and posed perfectly for Tracy, who'd gone first in a skirt covered with pencils and now stood in the aisle in front of the platform snapping pictures. As her fans clapped, and one woman, most likely Aunt Abigail, whistled, Jana made a slow turn then bowed and walked down the steps on the other end.

Next, it was Robin in her "wrap" dress—a beige wraparound with felt cutouts of chicken strips, pieces of lettuce, slices of tomato, and dollops of mayo sticking out. Carrie Ellis followed in her ball gown—a flowing pink dress covered in small rubber balls. When she left the stage, Whitney announced the pair Amy was sure would be the stars of the show. "Our next two models will stay toasty warm in their lovely blazers. Lisa is wearing a contemporary blazer, and Katerina Pasternak is modeling the vintage blazer she wore right here in 1955 at the first Faith Church Funny Fashion Show." Lisa stood back and let Katerina strut across the stage with the swagger of a twenty-year-old.

Amy poked her head out of the doorway to get a better look at the audience. Aunt Abigail rose to her feet, and everyone else took their cue from her. As cheers filled the room, Katerina stopped, did a graceful curtsy and then a slow turn, her face glowing.

When the room quieted, Whitney said, "Amy Allen is our final model, wearing an *egg*cellent yoke dress." Amy stepped out in her fried egg dress as Whitney read the script written sixty-eight years ago. "Perfect for when you have company over…easy dress for fixing breakfast when you don't want to *scramble* for something to wear. Notice the lovely front and back yoke. Our model will always keep her *sunny side up* in this frock."

"That concludes our funny fashion show. Please join us downstairs for dinner," Whitney said, and the audience clapped.

Amy stepped off the platform and into the small room where the worship team kept their mic stands, amplifiers, and other equipment. She gasped when she bumped into Katerina standing in the dark shadows. "The door is right there," she whispered.

The edge of the door leading to the backstage area was edged in glow-in-the-dark tape. Had she not seen it? Why hadn't Lisa stayed with her?

"I know," Katerina whispered back. "I told Lisa I wanted to wait here for you. This room reminded me of something. I was looking for Vi after our rehearsal for the fashion show. I found her in here. She was crying and she said something like, 'I've never, ever hated a person, but Mrs. Janvier is impossible.'"

The professor and his wife had been crossed off the wedding guest list. Because of this confrontation? "Do you know what Mrs. Janvier said to her?"

"She threatened her. Told her to keep her mouth shut or Professor Janvier would lose his job."

"Do you have any idea why?" Amy remembered Pop saying that Maura Childs suspected Sally of embezzling funds from the college. Did Violet know something about that?

"No. But it wasn't the first time I saw something. The day we went to Professor Janvier's house to show him the map, Mrs. Janvier answered the door and glared at Vi in a way that gave me chills. It was downright hateful. I thought maybe it was because she'd asked if we could meet with the professor in private. But when I look back, I think it was something more."

"Do you think she could have had anything to do with Violet's disappearance?"

"I wouldn't put it past her."

When Amy walked by Matt's room on her way to bed on Tuesday night, the glow beneath his sheet told her he was still awake and likely reading *Treasure Island*.

"Ahoy there, matey." She heard the book close as she sat on the edge of his bed.

He pulled the sheet down slowly. "Shiver me timbers!" He held the flashlight under his chin, giving his face ghoulish shadows around the reddish glow.

Amy grinned, loving the change in his mood. "I forgot to ask who won Settlers of Catan."

"Kai won, but I was close. I learned some new strategies. It was cool. Then we watched *Pan*. It's not like *Hook* or the other Peter Pan movies. It was pretty scary in parts, but I want to watch it again."

"Did you talk to them about vacation?"

"Yeah." Matt switched off his flashlight and set it on the nightstand. "I don't think Kai wants to go. He wants a real adventure, not one planned by people who are just luring you to their place so they can make money off you."

Luring? Oh boy. Kai was developing some great discerning skills. But Matt was too young to be thinking about those things. He'd been exposed to too much in his young life already. She wanted him to stay in a cocoon of protected innocence as long as possible. "I guess that's one way of looking at a dude ranch. Another way might be to see it as a place that provides jobs for all of their employees and gives families a fun way to spend more time with each other."

"Yeah. I guess. But hunting for treasure with you and Dr. Miles would be way more fun than a trail ride."

Amy rubbed her temple. Was everyone going to make her feel guilty for spending a day exploring with Miles? And was Matt really losing interest in their vacation plans, or was he just being momentarily influenced by Kai? For another month she could still cancel their reservations and only lose a small deposit. But right now she needed to address the immediate problem. "We don't know what we'll find on the islands. There's a lot of marshland, and it might not be safe."

"Then why are you going?" The question came from behind her.

Amy stretched out her arms, and Jana crawled onto her lap. She didn't fit quite as well as she had two years ago, but if she was still willing to sit on her lap, Amy would make it work. She rested her cheek against the soft curls that smelled of lemon verbena shampoo. "Why are you awake?"

"I had a dream and I woke up and I heard you talking."

"A good dream?"

"Kinda. A girl in my class got a pony and she showed us pictures, so I guess that's why I dreamed Natalie and me were riding horses in a big field with lots of flowers. I could ride really good and we went really fast. It was fun, but then the clouds turned all black and the wind started blowing and we got scared. When I woke up I wished I kept dreaming, 'cause then maybe I woulda ended up in Oz." She giggled into Amy's shoulder.

"Does riding horses still sound fun?" Amy didn't like the doubt in her voice, but she needed some reassurance that she wasn't going to be dragging her kids on an expensive vacation they didn't even want.

"Yes! But it would be a lot less scary if Natalie was there for real."

Amy was about to let out her frustration on a loud sigh when Matt said, "Nathan Tyler in my class takes riding lessons in Quincy. Could we take them before we go?"

Jana sat up. "That would be sooo much fun."

A jumble of emotions tumbled in Amy's chest. She was proud of Matt for reaching beyond his own feelings to support his sister, but he did that too often. He'd had years of being Jana's only protector. He needed to know he no longer had to carry that responsibility alone. She rested her hand lightly on his shoulder. "I think that would be a great idea. Let's make some plans tomorrow. But now it's time for all of us to go to sleep." She bent and kissed Matt's forehead. "Sweet dreams." Taking Jana by the hand, she led her back to her room and tucked her in.

Mom guilt. Why had no one warned her about this thing that followed her around like a black cloud and caused her to question almost everything? She crawled into bed, punched her pillow into the right configuration, turned off the light, and then sat up again and picked up her phone. She needed to think about something less frustrating before trying to sleep.

She went to newspapers.com, typed in *1954–1956 Canton, Missouri*, then added Sally Janvier's name. If only they'd had social media back then, she could have looked up all the gossip about the woman Violet had said was impossible to get along with. The woman who had accused her of…what exactly?

Several articles came up. Three articles mentioned Sally's work with the college auxiliary. Another contained a photo of Professor and Mrs. Antoine Janvier standing in front of the iconic Henderson Hall at Culver-Stockton College's centennial celebration in 1953.

The next was a human-interest piece about Antoine falling in love with his nurse and following her back to Missouri. Their 1946 wedding picture and one from May of 1956 were featured. So Antoine had not fled town when Violet disappeared. Of course, that didn't necessarily mean he had nothing to do with it. She read six articles and didn't find anything incriminating. But then she read a single line in a paper dated September 16, 1956. *Divorces granted: Sally Kennedy Janvier from Antoine R. Janvier.*

Chapter Nineteen

Amy shut off the light and tried again to force herself to sleep. Two minutes later, her eyes popped open. *Kennedy.* Was Sally's middle name Kennedy? It hadn't said "née Kennedy" like she'd expect it to if it was her maiden name. But she couldn't shake the idea that Sally Janvier might have been related to Don Kennedy—the man Katerina had said was in love with Violet. The man who had made Violet jump out of *River Dancer*.

She couldn't sleep until she found out more. She typed in *Sally Kennedy, Canton, Missouri*.

Nothing. Until she took out *Canton*. In the late thirties, a Sally Kennedy had acted the lead roles in several Monticello High School plays. Monticello was about ten miles west of Canton. A little more digging revealed a picture of Sally Kennedy in 1943 wearing a nurse's uniform and posing with a group of other nurses about to board a train bound for New York City and then on to France. They would be serving on the battlefront with the Red Cross. Definitely the right Sally. Now to find out if she had a connection to Don.

It only took a few minutes of searching to find out that Katerina was right. Don and his wife Muriel now lived in Canton. She found the address and looked up the street view. A newer condo. She also found the name Donald Kennedy in an obituary for Damon

Kennedy, Jr., his brother. Since no other siblings were listed, she assumed Damon was the half-brother Katerina had mentioned. And if Damon was a junior, named after their father, he was likely the oldest. The next line made her sit up straighter.

Damon was preceded in death by his parents, Damon Kennedy Sr. and Zeda (née Anderson), and aunt and uncle, Dr. Antoine and Sally (née Kennedy) Janvier.

Did that mean Sally Janvier's brother was Damon Jr. and Don Kennedy's father?

Amy felt like someone was squeezing her head, putting pressure on her temples and making it hard to think. What was her next step?

If Don was the same age as Violet, he'd be in his late eighties. Hopefully, he was still in possession of all his faculties.

Because Amy intended to pay him a visit tomorrow.

She fell asleep and spent a restless night drifting between scrolling to-do lists and dreams of being shipwrecked on an island in the Mississippi River and finding a chest full of gold that turned out to be millions of little gold stars like the ones she gave her students to put in their assignment books when they finished a worksheet.

When her alarm went off, the light shining through her curtains was much brighter than Amy felt. A hot shower began the reviving process, and a shot of espresso with a couple of fried eggs completed it. She woke the kids and fed them a better-than-usual breakfast of ham and cheese omelets while she made sandwiches for what Matt had begrudgingly dubbed "Mom and Dr. Miles's Great Adventure Without Kids."

"I still don't see why we can't go," he said for the fifth time over breakfast. "At least me and Colton."

"Colton and I," Amy corrected, just to get a rise out of her son. "'I don't see why Colton *and I* can't go.'"

"Well, I don't!"

His angry face was adorable. Amy couldn't resist using one of her father's favorite lines. "You're so cute when you're mad." This brought a growl. "We've already talked about this. If the island is safe, we'll take all of you out there sometime."

"Yeah. After you find the treasure."

"I promise we'll re-bury some of the gold doubloons and pieces of eight for you to find."

Matt grumbled under his breath and kept up a running commentary on the unfairness of the day all the way to school, but Amy could see, in the rearview mirror, the smiles he exchanged with Jana. It didn't take his little sister long to join his tirade.

"We never get to do anything fun," she said, whining through her nose. "The grownups get all the adventures, and we have to go to school." Her bottom lip stuck out impossibly far. Matt gave her a thumbs-up.

Time to call their bluff. Amy eased on the brake and pulled the car to the curb a block from school. "Okay. I give. You guys can come along. There won't be room in the boat for you with all of our treasure hunting gear, but Dr. Miles has swim rings. We can pull you behind. Might get a little chilly, but you guys are tough. I'll call the school and let your teachers know you won't be there."

She pretended to tap in a number. "Hi, Kelly, it's Amy. Hey, we decided to take Matt and Jana and Natalie and Colton on our trip today, so they won't be in school." She paused, giving imaginary Kelly time to answer. "Jana and Natalie won't mind missing that.

What's a pumpkin cupcake and popcorn and a movie compared to tromping through a swamp in November?" Another pause. "Yeah, I heard the mosquitoes were thick out there this year, but I'm sure it's too cold for them now. Probably, anyway. Snakes? I doubt they're poisonous." She glanced in the mirror, watching Jana's pout morph into a grimace. "Nah, Matt wasn't all that interested in going to the middle school to see the Thanksgiving play. And I think he's lost interest in basketball. Especially when he has the choice of spending the day being wet and cold on—"

"Okay! Stop! We surrender."

In most circumstances, she would have reprimanded her son and daughter for sticking their tongues out at their mother. But not this time.

Miles hoisted a canvas bag into the boat. Amy handed him the cooler she'd packed with ham and cheese sandwiches, potato chips, oranges, snickerdoodles, and cans of soda, and then held out two large thermoses, one containing coffee, the other vegetable soup. Even though there wasn't a cloud in the sky, after several hours in the conditions she'd threatened her children with—tromping around on a swampy island in mid-fifties temperatures—they'd want something hot.

When the last of their gear was on board, she unwrapped the mooring lines from the cleats on the dock. Miles held out his hand, and she stepped onto the deck. When he didn't let go of her hand, she looked up into sunlit brown eyes gazing at her. His usual close-to-the-surface smile was gone. She couldn't quite define that expression. He seemed to be searching her face for confirmation... of what? The intensity unnerved her. "What?"

Her question dispelled whatever had caused the moment of seriousness, and his teasing smile returned. "You sure do know how to dress the part."

"What's that supposed to mean?" Amy looked down at an outfit that would have made Whitney—and Tracy, and probably most women she knew—cringe. She wore waterproof hiking boots and flannel-lined jeans with red plaid fabric showing through several holes. The ragged cuffs and hem of a long-sleeved waffle-weave pink shirt peaked out from a sweatshirt with YOU CAN'T SCARE ME, I'M A TEACHER! printed on the front. A fifteen-pocket tan cargo vest borrowed from Jeff, garden gloves that had seen better days, and two short braids poking out of a lime green stocking cap with ear flaps, completed the ensemble. Jeff's chest waders were in the canvas bag.

"It means you're adorable." Miles, whose jacket, jeans, and boots made him look like he'd just stepped out of a clothing ad in *Field & Stream* magazine, brushed a kiss across her forehead. He winked then sat in the captain's chair and started the motor. In minutes they were heading downriver. It would take them less than an hour to reach Teal Island, but they'd decided to stop at each place that had been numbered on Professor Conway's pencil-drawn map.

Amy sat on the bench seat closest to Miles. "I'm imagining I'm Violet. It's before dawn, and I'm terrified because somebody has taken me against my will."

"How did they do that? Drag you kicking and screaming from your bed, but no one in the house heard? Drug you? Threaten you?"

"That had to be it. She was threatened or blackmailed. Did she bring the boat keys, or had someone made copies?"

Miles stroked his chin. "The water's pretty shallow here. If you were being held against your will, would you try to jump overboard?"

"I'd be worried about the current. And what if I had a gun pointed at me?"

"Or they'd threatened to hurt someone you cared about if you didn't cooperate." Miles increased the boat's speed, and a fine mist sprayed over the bow. "The note Aunt Ruth and Aunt Abigail found with the dolls sounded like someone was warning your grandmother to keep quiet."

Amy nodded. "They could have been threatening to hurt Lenny or Grandma and Grandpa and their children." Had her father's life been in danger? Strange to consider the possibility that if Violet's story had turned out differently, Amy, Tracy, Robin, and their children might not even be here. "I wish we'd had a chance to ask Violet some questions before we did this."

"But that might have spoiled all our fun. What if she said there never was any treasure, or someone had already gotten to it so there was no use in looking?"

"Good point." She smiled at him, basking in the warmth of a gaze that made her wish they had much longer than four hours to spend on the river together. She went back to imagining she was Violet. Her father had died six weeks before. She'd found an old map with numbers and an X on it. She'd shown it to several friends and a professor who confirmed that it was probably at least a hundred years old. Then what? Someone who knew about the map, probably Don Kennedy, was holding her hostage, making her steal a boat so they could find the treasure buried on Teal Island. Years later, after his brother died, Don moved back to Canton. Why? Because his brother was the only one who knew what Don had done to Violet? How could a man live with that kind of guilt? And had he found the treasure?

"Catch me up on your imagining." Miles grinned at the use of the word he'd borrowed from Tracy. "Figure it out yet?"

She laid out all her conjectures. "So much doesn't make sense. Violet married Lenny and he changed their last name, so maybe Don never knew she survived. But he didn't change his name. Even if he'd moved out of Canton, someone could have found him. Why didn't she turn him in?"

"Fear. If we're right about him, he sounds like a dangerous guy. If he'd tried to kill her once, he'd do it again. I can see why she would have been afraid to face him in court."

"That's not at all the way the Pasternaks described him. He sounded like a fun-loving prankster. Everybody liked Don, they said."

"Maybe that was just a facade. Or maybe greed changed him." Miles pointed to the zippered pouch Amy had laid on the seat beside her. "Read," he said. "We have forty minutes to find out what we're looking for."

Amy felt a shiver of anticipation as she pulled out the sheaf of papers. Even though William Conway's introduction had described Sea Dog Sam as a bent old man, his name implied that at one time he had likely been tough as nails, maybe even feared by other pirates. She cleared her throat and began reading where she'd left off.

> *I hid in the brush for what must have been an hour, listening in on their plans. The man with sausage fingers dipped a stick in black liquid and drew on the hide. He said that Blackbeard's treasure was buried near New Detroit, under a rock formation that looked like a bridge. When he said, "I may be an illegitimate no-account, but I swear on the grave of me recently departed father, Jean Baptiste Lafitte, that what I say is true," I gasped, and in short order found myself surrounded by two pistols, a musket, and a cutlass.*

Amy bit her bottom lip. How she wished Matt was here, reading this with her. "If this is true, my dad's nanny's father knew someone personally who ran with Blackbeard. It's like a connection, like I'm directly connected to one of the most infamous pirates that ever lived. And maybe we'll find his treasure!"

The response from Miles was an even wider dimple-revealing smile. "Why aren't you writing fantasy books? I'm sure you're the best first-grade teacher that ever lived, but I think you may have missed your true calling."

Her face warming, Amy turned away. "You're not the first person to suggest that. I promise that if we find Blackbeard's treasure, I will write our story, and I'll split the royalties with you. Of course, we'll be so rich by then we won't even need that money. Maybe I'll start a nonprofit scholarship for kids who have almost-direct connections to people who knew real pirates back in the day."

Miles laughed. "In other words, your kids."

"And yours. You know me, and my dad knew Violet, and Violet's dad knew Sea Dog Sam, who knew Blackbeard, so your kids will be eligible."

There was something about being able to make Dr. Miles Anderson laugh that warmed her to her toes. And brought out the silly side of her, something that had gotten a bit lost in all of her recent busyness.

"No more nonprofits. Promise me."

She feigned a frustrated sigh. "Fine. But it will be on your conscience that all of those kids with almost-direct connections to pirates won't get a decent college education."

"I'll deal with the guilt." He pointed ahead. "That's Willow Island."

Amy bent down, reached into her bag, and pulled out two things Matt had handed her, with a genuine smile, right before getting out of the car at school. His spyglass. And an eye patch.

Patch in place, she lifted the brass telescope to her other eye and shouted, "Ahoy there, matey, land ho!"

Miles turned, opened his mouth, closed it again, then laughed so hard he almost lost control of the boat.

June 20, 1955

Last night, after I closed Violet's diary, I leaned back against her headboard and heard something metal drop to the floor. When I got down on my hands and knees, I found a CSC class ring. A man's ring, quite large and heavy. With the initials DJK. Donald J. Kennedy. At first I thought maybe Don had given it to Violet, but when I looked closer, there was a tiny shard of glass clinging to the bedspread right above it. I believe it must have been the thing that broke the window.

It was obvious when the group was here that Don had a bit of a crush on Vi, but he was one of Lenny's best friends. I assumed he would soon get a handle on his emotions. He was dating Ellen, after all, and I sensed maybe she was aware of the one-sided attraction. It's hard to accept that Howard and I could have been so wrong about him. The flirtations seemed innocent and fit his gregarious nature. He was always telling jokes and recounting hilarious predicaments he had gotten himself into. I'm in shock thinking he's probably the one who took her away. But for what purpose? Until I found the ring, I was sure this all had something to do with the treasure map. Now I'm not so sure. Dear God, protect our Violet!

Howard and I gave Violet's diary to the police. They are searching for Don.

Chapter Twenty

Miles trolled slowly along the western side of Willow Island while Amy read aloud what she'd found on her phone about the Great River National Wildlife Refuge that encompassed all the islands they hoped to visit. "'It protects more than eleven thousand acres of the river, stretching a hundred and twenty miles north of St. Louis. In 1998, it was designated as a globally Important Bird Area.'" As if on cue, a flock of birds landed on the surface of the river about fifty feet ahead of them.

"Blue-winged teals," Amy said. "They're on their way south from Canada or Alaska."

Miles cut the motor. "I didn't realize you were an ornithologist."

She laughed. "I only know a few of the migratory birds that follow the river every year. I think I remember these because I love the name. I wonder if Teal Island was named for them."

They sat in silence and watched the birds dip their heads underwater to pull up vegetation.

Amy looked around, seeing nothing but green, orange, red, and gold on every side and mirrored in the smooth surface of the river. No signs of civilization. "Imagine we're in a birchbark canoe, the first Europeans to see this place."

She waited for a response then glanced back at Miles, whose thoughts seemed miles away. After a moment, he blinked, as if clearing his mental screen, and looked a bit flustered. "Sorry. Just… thinking. I suppose you don't want me messing with your birchbark vision by telling you these islands were probably created when the US Army Conservation Corps started putting in locks and dams in the thirties."

"No, I don't want— Wait. If that's true, then this"—she pulled out their copy of William Conway's map—"couldn't have been drawn by the man with sausage fingers in 1854." She stared at the dimple, squinting her eyes at Miles. "You knew this all along."

Miles held up both hands in defense. "No, I didn't. I did some research last night. There would have been islands, but probably not these."

Amy tapped on her maps app and typed in *Willow Island*. The aerial view appeared longer and more pointed than the one on the pencil drawing. One spot of land identified on Conway's map as Diamond Island was no longer there. "Teal Island is a lot smaller now."

"Probably means the treasure is underwater." Mirth glinted in his eyes.

"Funny." Amy studied the small green oval, enlarging it with her fingers. "I think there's a clearing right in the center. Right where the X is on the map." If she searched, she might be able to find a river map from the mid-1900s and maybe one from a hundred years before that. But she didn't want to. She didn't want the magic spoiled by finding out it hadn't been drawn by pirates after all. She sighed. "Let's not overthink this. Let's just follow the map the best we can and have fun with it."

"I'm with you." Miles started the motor, and the flock of teals rose in one flapping, squawking mass. They rounded the southern end of Willow Island but couldn't find a place shallow enough to anchor the boat and walk onto shore. In the next half hour, they found the same to be true of Hogback Island. Only Teal Island, the one that really mattered, was left.

"There." Miles pointed to a strip of sand along the east side of the small island. He navigated close enough that they'd be able to drop anchor and have easy access through about three feet of water. "Get your waders out, mate."

She almost fell twice as she stepped into the too-big boots and pulled up the attached PVC-coated bib. Miles, who had made gearing-up look easy, helped shorten the elastic straps that crisscrossed her back. Though they were called chest waders, the top of the bib came almost to her chin. They filled packs with trowels, metal detecting pointers, and headphones. Amy felt like a weighted-down, wobbly penguin when Miles hoisted her pack onto her shoulders. She looked at the boat ladder. "Not a chance I'm going to do this gracefully."

"Grace is not required. I'll go first." Miles climbed into the water. "Hand me the metal detectors. I'll get them to shore and come back for you."

No way was she going to play the role of helpless female. She waited until Miles left the boat then turned around, put one foot on the metal ladder, grabbed the curved handles, and began to lower herself. Easy, one step at a time. All went well until she stepped into the water and let go of the rail. The pull of the current caught her by surprise, and the weight of her pack yanked her backwards. Just as she was about to go under, strong arms caught her, righted her, and held her close. Close enough to feel the laughter rumbling in his chest. And then he pulled away, looking into her face with that same unnerving seriousness. She was about to say something silly to break the tension when he lowered his head, resting his forehead on hers. "I love you." His voice was low and rough. "Thank you."

Her breath caught, and for a moment she had to concentrate on expanding her lungs to let in air. Strange that just a matter of days earlier she hadn't been sure she was ready to hear those three little words. "Thank me for what?"

"For giving me a second chance."

"I think it's the other way around. Thank *you*." Her voice cracked. "And I love you too."

His fingertips trailed along her cheek. He lifted her chin and then lowered his lips to hers. When he finally pulled away, he whispered, "Ready for the adventure of a lifetime?"

That seemed a bit dramatic, but she nodded. Miles kept one hand clamped on her arm until they stepped out of the water and she found her footing on the hard-packed sand. She waddled to a toppled log to sit on to exchange her waders for hiking boots so she could walk like a woman rather than an awkward arctic bird. She put on her backpack, Miles attached her metal detector to it, and then she did the same for him. When they were ready, she said in a hushed voice, "Let the exploring begin."

They stood for several minutes, scanning the narrow beach, looking for a way through the underbrush. Miles gripped his machete and began making wide arcs, clearing a swath through the tangle as he walked. About ten feet into the dense growth, he stopped. "I think there used to be a path here." He stepped back and turned sideways so Amy could see around him.

"You're right." The underbrush was still thick, but there seemed to be a corridor where no larger trees grew. As they fought their way through, Amy unzipped her vest, grateful for the cool air. She couldn't imagine hacking through this in July, when Violet disappeared. The heat would have been oppressive, the swarms of biting mosquitoes enough to drive a person mad.

They struggled at a snail's pace for about twenty minutes and then suddenly broke into a green meadow. "The clearing!" Amy said. She looked around. The peaceful feeling she'd had an hour earlier was gone. Now she couldn't shake the uneasy impression that they were trespassing. It didn't make sense. This wasn't private land. "Let's walk out there," she said, pointing. "Do you think this is a natural clearing?"

"Watch for signs of felled trees." Miles took a step and almost tripped. "Like that one." He crouched down, examining the decayed remains of a tree stump. He sifted through a pile of wood chips then held up a piece about half the size of his hand. "It's been cut."

Amy moved closer. One edge was splintered, the other perfectly straight. "Like a mini version of the *River Dancer* name board."

Miles nodded. "Wish we had some way of figuring out when it was cut, or even what it was cut with. I can't tell if it was an axe or a modern-day chainsaw. It definitely wasn't done in the 1800s. Possibly in the fifties. Or maybe much more recently. Where's an expert on the rate of wood decay when you need one?"

They walked in silence, around several similar crumbling tree stumps, to the middle of the clearing. According to the aerial map, this was the exact center of the island. "I can't imagine that pirates would bury treasure right out in the open," Amy said.

"Me neither. But I could imagine someone years later clearing all the trees while trying to locate the treasure." Miles rubbed his chin. "Where are the logs?"

"Good question." Someone had chopped down trees, but there was no sign of them. "Maybe they used them to build a boat."

"Or a house." Miles pointed north.

Amy looked in that direction, but it took her a minute to see the edge of a moss-covered roof between two blazing maples. Had they come here in the middle of the summer, it would likely have been completely camouflaged. Her pulse speeding up, she walked ahead of Miles. Was this why she'd had the feeling they were trespassing? "What if someone lives here?"

"Then they're squatters and they won't take kindly to us nosin' around. Are you prepared to meet your maker if'n we find ourselves starin' down the barrel of a loaded shotgun?"

Amy rolled her eyes then stopped in her tracks and swept her hand out, telling him to go ahead of her. "I don't want to deprive you of the opportunity to protect a damsel in distress."

Miles held out his machete and leaned forward like he was heading into battle with bayonet drawn. "Never fear, m'lady. I am here."

An overgrown path led from the clearing to the structure that appeared to be about twelve feet square. "House" was too grand a word for the small shack. They approached it slowly, trying to not make a sound. Made of faded split logs with moss for chinking, it sat on a foundation of round field stones. A door opening, sans door, faced the clearing. Instead of windows, there were several narrow spaces between logs, just wide enough to look out. Or slide a gun barrel through.

"Hello?" Miles called out, making Amy jump.

No answer. They stepped closer. No footprints marred the dirt around it. Miles lifted his foot and stepped carefully inside. He unfastened a flashlight hooked to his belt. "Watch your step. The floor could be rotten."

It was. Right in the center, a hole gaped. But the boards around the edges seemed solid. Amy took a moment to let her eyes adjust. Several shafts of light from the narrow openings cut across the room, which was empty except for some flat boards about six inches wide and six feet long lying on top of four thick, square chunks of wood. A bed?

"Somebody lived here," Miles said. "Who, and how long ago?"

Amy turned on her flashlight, aiming it at the hole in the floor. She eased a step closer. "I don't think this just caved in on its own."

"You're right." Miles leaned down. With both lights trained on the broken boards, it was clear to see hack marks likely made by an axe or hatchet. "Someone was searching for something." He moved several boards aside, lay flat on his belly, and aimed his light into the hole. "It's only about three feet deep. Looks like nothing but dirt and cobwebs, but the dirt has been disturbed. I'm going down there."

"Are you sure? There might be creepy crawlies."

Miles rolled on his side and gave her a deadpan look. "Snakes. Why did it have to be snakes?"

His flat, Indiana Jones tone was perfect. Amy laughed, thinking, not for the first time that day, how much joy he'd brought into her life in the past few months. "I'm not sucking out the venom if you get bit."

"Wow. That's harsh." He sat up and took off his backpack. "If I don't return, you can have my bug collection. And my kids." He winked at her, eased his feet into the hole, and then slowly lowered until he was on his knees. She handed him his metal detector and watched as he swung it awkwardly back and forth in the cramped space. After a minute, his head popped up. "Nothing. Not even a nail."

As he climbed out, Amy swept her light around the walls, looking for anything that might give a hint of who had once lived there. In the corners, the logs were joined by notches. "I think it was built without nails." Someone had built this by hand with primitive tools. Who? And where did they store things? There were no shelves or cupboards or even hooks on the wall. And no fireplace. How did he, she, or they, cook and keep warm? She arced the beam up to the crude rafters overhead. Cobwebs. Dried leaves. But then, a tiny spot of red caught her eye. "Miles." She stepped over him. "Can you reach that?"

He stood, dusted off his knees, and looked up. "I see it, but..." He stretched then shook his head. "So close. I need another two inches." Without explanation, he dropped down on all fours. "Climb on."

Amy stared at his strong, flat back. She knew he could support her weight. What she didn't know was if she had the coordination to balance on it. "Okay." She held her breath as she stepped up. Keeping her gaze straight ahead, she rose, straightening her legs and then her torso. Finally feeling steady enough to look up, she reached over her head with one hand until her fingers touched something metal. A little higher and she was able to rest her hand on a slightly curved top. Letting out her breath, she brought her other hand up and grasped the object. Rectangular, about six by twelve inches, and maybe five inches high. A box. Rough with rust. Beneath her fingertips, she felt small hinges. Her breath became shallow as she lifted it off the beam and heard a distinct rattle. It could only be one thing. Coins.

"I th-think we found the treasure."

Chapter Twenty-One

"It's heavy." Amy followed Miles back to the edge of the clearing where sunlight landed on the box in her hands. After brushing off a thick layer of dust and flakes of rust, she was able to make out words. *Olde English Curve Cut Tobacco.*

"Maybe not Blackbeard's treasure," Miles said wryly.

"Oh ye of little faith." She shook the can. "Hear that? Gold doubloons. And a gold bullion. Or two."

"Or about seventy-five cents in quarters and a couple of rocks."

"I am not going to let you rain on my parade." Just because he was right that it didn't sound like a lot of coins didn't mean they weren't worth anything. And there was something else in the box, something heavy. Amy got down on her knees, set the box on a flat, partially buried rock, and tried to budge the top, but it was rusted shut. Miles knelt beside her then picked it up and banged the lid against the rock. A shower of rust particles fell to the ground. He pushed up on the front of the cover with one thumb, and it popped open about an inch. He handed the tin back to Amy.

Before opening it, she locked eyes with Miles. "What do you think is in it?"

"Besides the rocks and quarters? Maybe another map. Leading to another map and then another... Because a nice pirate left these here. He didn't want to hurt anyone trying to steal his booty, just drive them nuts."

Amy looked up to the cloudless sky. "Okay. I'm ready." The tiny hinges whined as she opened the lid. A folded piece of yellowed paper sat on top. She lifted it out of the way. Miles was almost right. Five coins rested on top of what appeared to be a once-white handkerchief. A 1928 buffalo nickel, three wheat pennies, and two liberty quarters, one from 1926, the other from 1924. One by one, she handed them to Miles.

"Bet these are worth enough to buy us ice cream on the way home."

Amy wrinkled her nose at him. "It was never about the money. These are clues. The money is all pre-1930. It could have belonged to Sea Dog Sam."

"If, indeed, he was a real person." Though he tried to keep a straight face, the skin around his eyes crinkled.

"Stop being a downer."

He yanked on one of her braids. "I like irritating you."

"I've gathered that." Now it was her turn to stifle a smile. In truth, she couldn't think of a single person she'd rather be irritated by. "Get serious." She looked back in the tin and grasped the hanky by the edge of one corner, using her thumb and forefinger.

"If Blackbeard blew his nose on that, the germs would be dead by now."

"Ew. That's disgusting." She was tempted to drop it, but continued to lift it slowly. *Clunk.* Something heavy fell out of the handkerchief.

A gun. Not much longer than Amy's hand.

Miles picked it up.

"I don't like seeing that," Amy said quietly.

"What's the paper say?" he asked.

She'd almost forgotten about the paper in her hand. She unfolded it and held it out so they could read it together.

June 26, 1955

Dear Vi,

I don't suppose you will ever believe that I wasn't the one to tell Damon about the map. I have no idea how he found out. I overheard him talking to someone, making a plan to break in and force you to give them the map and the keys to the Allens' boat. When I confronted him, he threatened to hurt you if I told anyone. I had to offer to go along to protect you. Damon would have killed you, I am convinced of that. I need you to know that I would have taken a bullet for you if it came to that, and it almost did. I wrestled the gun out of his hand while you swam to shore, then hit him over the head with it. That was when I made my escape. I swam to Teal Island. Maybe an hour later, I heard the boat motor in the distance. I expected him to come after me, or after the treasure, but it's been a week, and he hasn't.

I'm staying on the island while I figure out what to do next. I can't go back home until I know he's behind bars. I pray you are safe and that you called the police and they have apprehended Damon. Believe me when I say I want the best for you and Len.

I know you will probably never see this, but it makes me feel better to have written it down.

Yours always,

Don

Nothing Gold Can Stay

Amy ran the metal detector back and forth a few inches above the ground as she walked in widening circles around the cabin. They'd covered every inch of the inside and found no metal of any kind.

Miles scanned the clearing. After twenty minutes, neither of them had found anything. Had Don built the cabin? Would a college kid have had the skill and perseverance to build a structure like this with just what he'd found on the island? Or were Professor Conway's stories about meeting Sea Dog Sam on Teal Island all true? Had the man who claimed to have known Samuel Clemens, who'd watched a band of pirates draw a map leading to Blackbeard's treasure, walked the ground she was now walking?

So many questions. Did Vi ever hear Don's explanation? Did she ever know he wasn't the one after the treasure? And then another thought hit. Did Don know Violet had survived and that she was still alive?

Amy's foot hit something hidden in the weeds, and she almost tripped. A circle of rocks the size of bowling balls was camouflaged by tall grass. Was this where the person had cooked? And what did they cook? Fish, maybe. She'd seen one rabbit since they'd gotten off the boat. It wasn't likely there had ever been any large game on this tiny bit of land. Did the person leave the island to get food?

A loud, clear tone warbling through her headphones interrupted the stream of questions. She slowed, covering smaller patches of ground as she zeroed in on the sound. This was different than any she'd heard before. Not iron, definitely not aluminum. She looked at the number on her gauge and dared to hope. Dropping to her knees, she ripped off the headphones and pulled her pointer out of the holder attached to her belt. She jabbed it at the weed-covered ground in several spots. *Beep. Beep.* The sound got louder and faster, and the pointer vibrated in her hand. After slipping out of her backpack, she took out the foldable shovel, straightened it, and dug a U-shaped flap in the sod. Then she knelt again, pulled out the plug of dirt, and ran the pointer across it. Not there. But when she directed the end of the pointer to the center of the hole, the sound pierced the stillness.

Out of the corner of her eye, she saw Miles loping toward her. As he dropped to the ground beside her, she scooped out a mound of dirt with her trowel and checked it again. The piercing tone was even louder. She set the trowel aside and began sifting through the dirt with her fingers. She felt something stringy, about six inches long. Thinking it was a root, she was about to toss it aside, but she took a second look. "It's a piece of leather."

"Probably a drawstring for a pirate's treasure pouch. The doubloons should be right under it, matey."

He was mocking her, but she didn't care. Because there *was* something. A tiny glint of something shiny. She grabbed it between her fingers and rubbed the dirt caking it.

Flat and round. A button. Or a coin?

Amy held her breath as Miles dug out his spray bottle and misted it.

Gold. Unmistakable gold.

He sprayed it again then let out a long, low whistle as muddy water dripped off the surface, revealing Lady Liberty's profile and a date. 1820.

Holding the coin tight in her fist, Amy threw her arms around Miles. "Say it. Say I was right."

His laughter rolled over her. "You were right. There is pirate treasure, or somebody's treasure, on Teal Island."

"There might be more." She put her pointer back in the hole and the same loud, clear beep sounded. Repeating the sifting motions all over again, she prodded until she picked up another round object, this one smaller, not completely round, and with a hole in the middle. She held it out for Miles to spray. A tiny bit of green glinted in the sunlight, and Amy gasped. A small, square-cut emerald perched on top of a gold band, twisted to look like it had been braided. "It's beautiful. I wonder how old it is."

Miles took it from her. His expression turned sober. The playfulness of moments earlier was gone. Instead of sharing the astonished wonder she felt, he simply stared at it.

"Miles?"

He didn't answer. His Adam's apple bobbed. The hand that held the ring began to tremble.

"Miles? What is it? Do you recognize it? What are you thinking?"

He shook his head. His lips parted, but he didn't say anything. This time, his swallow was audible, but his face appeared frozen. He'd been acting strange off and on all morning. Was he having a stroke?

Her pulse sped up. She touched his arm. "Are you okay? You're scaring me. Do you feel sick?"

He answered with a slow nod, but no words. His Adam's apple bobbed again.

"Do you need to lie down? Maybe you should drink some water." She turned to get her bottle out of her pack, but he grabbed her arm.

"I only need"—the faintest of smiles softened his features—"you."

"What?" He wasn't making sense. Panic surged through her. "Can you stand? We need to get back to the boat. I don't want to scare you, but confusion can be a sign of a stroke."

Another almost imperceptible nod. "It is. It's a sign."

Her chest tightened. For a moment she thought she might black out. But she had to stay clearheaded, had to get him back to the boat. Could she drive it herself? Where was the nearest hospital? "Try to stand."

He shook his head. "You stand."

"Okay." That made sense. She could help him up. She pushed up from the ground and held both arms out to him.

He grabbed her left hand and stared into her eyes with an intensity that sent panic surging through her. "All day, I've been asking God for a sign. And He just gave it to me." He held up the dirt-encrusted ring.

And slipped it on her dirt-encrusted finger.

"Amy Allen, I want to spend the rest of my life laughing through crazy adventures with you and your kids and my kids. Will you marry me?"

Her gasp echoed off the trees surrounding the clearing, and she dropped back to her knees and into his arms. His padded vest almost drowned out her answer, spoken with a sob of relief mingled with surprise and joy. "Yes. Absolutely yes!"

Chapter Twenty-Two

Don Kennedy sat with a plaid blanket over his lap. He had a full head of snow-white hair. His body was lean, his face lined in ways that said he had known sorrow. One hand rested on the tin box. "I never thought I'd see this again. I thought about going back for it, but then I decided I just wanted to leave that chapter of my life behind. It's all in there? The gun?"

"Yes," Miles said.

Don's eyes misted as he picked up the folded note and read silently, his lips forming the words he'd written sixty-eight years ago. His wife, Muriel, handed him a tissue, and he set the paper on his lap, took off his glasses, and wiped his eyes. "So long ago," he whispered.

Miles, sitting next to Amy on a gray love seat, rested his fingertips on her now clean left hand and tapped the sparkling emerald ring that, in a miracle only God could have orchestrated, fit as if it had been made for her. She told herself not to get too attached, since she might not be able to keep it. Miles had contacted the Department of Natural Resources before they left the island, asking if they should leave it where they'd found it. He'd been told to mark the spot and bring the ring into their office on Monday. It was likely they wouldn't get an answer for several days. But she'd enjoy it as long as she could, all with the memory of her anything-but-traditional proposal.

As they waited for Don to begin his story, Amy said a silent prayer, asking God to give him strength.

After a shaky breath, he began. "I first met Damon, my half-brother, when I was thirteen. He was two years older, the product of a lawful marriage. I was the illegitimate son. The only thing my father ever gave me was his last name. When the truth came out, Damon's mother left. Neither of us knew how to handle our anger. I resented Damon for being raised in an intact family. He resented me just for existing and bursting his illusion that he had a happy home. We were both angry that we'd missed out on growing up together, being brothers."

Don took a sip of the tea Muriel set in front of him. "In my senior year of college, I shared an apartment with a couple of friends. Damon lost his job and asked if he could move in with us. I thought it would be great to finally get to know him. I had no idea the kind of people he was involved with. One night he started packing up his stuff, mumbling about how he had to find the treasure and get away from 'them.' A few minutes later I overheard him on the phone saying he was going to break into the Allens' house and force Violet to give him the map, then steal their boat, find the treasure, and hand over whatever he found. I confronted him, and he shoved me out of his way. He wouldn't tell me how he found out about the map. He said if I warned Vi, he or the men he owed money to would hurt both of us and anyone we cared about. Then he told me he had a ten-thousand-dollar gambling debt. In today's dollars that would be about a hundred thousand." He stopped a moment to let the amount register. "He planned on finding the treasure and heading to New Orleans, and he didn't intend to pay off his debt unless the men who were after him found him.

"I had to warn Vi, so I convinced Damon to wait until dawn, when it would be getting light and he'd be sobered up and could think straight. I said I'd help him if he gave me a cut of the treasure. He went to bed, and I called Vi and told her to pack up and run. I prayed she wouldn't be there when we got there, but she was. That's when I found out Damon had a gun and he intended to take Vi as a hostage."

Don set his cup on the table, eased back against the chair cushion, and closed his eyes. "I'm sorry."

"Take your time," Amy said. "We know you would never have intentionally put Violet in danger."

"Never," he whispered. He ran a hand over his eyes. "I didn't know it at the time, but my brother was schizophrenic."

Amy's heart went out to the poor man who seemed to age before her eyes as his story unfolded. She still had so many questions, but she didn't know if he'd be able to continue. As Don closed his eyes again, she came up with a plan. "Have you had any communication with Violet?"

His eyes shot open. "Communication?" He shook his head. "I know she made it safely to Lenny's grandparents' house. That's all I know. I have no idea what happened to her after that."

Amy scooted to the end of her chair and touched his hand. "She has had a good life. She married Lenny, and they had a daughter."

"She's still…" His shoulders shook.

"Yes. Violet is still alive. And she needs to hear the whole story. From you."

As they drove away from Terry and Robin's after leaving the kids' Adoption Day gift in their safekeeping, Amy leaned her head against Miles's shoulder. She hadn't told Robin about the proposal. That was a secret for later tonight when the women gathered to set tables for tomorrow. "I wish I had nothing else on my mind right now but dreaming of our life together."

Miles didn't answer. When he parked the car two blocks from the school, she turned to face him. His cheek moved, as if he were literally biting back words. "What are you thinking?"

His chest rose and fell in a heavy sigh. "I'm thinking about how to say what I want to say without bruising your beautiful, capable, independent spirit."

She chuckled. "My spirit does not bruise all that easily, Dr. Anderson, and if you do break your Hippocratic Oath and cause harm, I'm quite sure you know just the right remedy. So say it."

His smile warmed her far more than the air from the Jeep's heater. "Is it chivalrous, or chauvinistic, to offer to help my bride-to-be financially? Meaning, you don't need to feel pressured to launch your store on Monday unless you want to." When she opened her mouth to protest, he held up a hand. "If it were up to me, we'd get married today, but I want you to have everything you've ever dreamed of. That said, I'm hoping we will be wed and sufficiently honeymooned by the time that vacation you're planning comes around. Which means, we will all go. Right?"

Her brain hadn't had time to process that far into the future. "I guess it would mean that." Which would make both of her children absolutely ecstatic.

"Well, then, I hereby insist that my wedding gift to my new family be a family vacation to Golden Sky Dude Ranch."

A sob rose from Amy's chest. As the stress she'd put on herself for weeks began to cascade off her shoulders, the pent-up tears she'd been holding back couldn't be restrained. And the arms engulfing her were a promise that, even though her parenting responsibilities were about to double, she'd no longer have to shoulder them alone.

When she finally had her emotions under control, at least for a few more minutes, Miles pulled into the long line of cars waiting in front of the school. Amy blotted her palms against her jeans. This was the first time they'd pick up the kids together. In fact, it was the only time she'd picked up Matt and Jana in front of the school. She'd texted Sara and asked her to tell them to look for Miles's car when they came out.

Miles drummed the steering wheel with both hands, clearly as nervous as she was. "They're going to love this, right?"

"If they don't, we go to Plan B."

"Which is?"

"Giving them their adoption gift early."

The lines of his jaw relaxed. "I'm marrying you for your brilliance, you know."

"And here I thought it was for my style sense."

The bell rang, and Amy sat up straight in her seat.

"Chicken."

She laughed. "A certain measure of decorum is required for a teacher."

"Until after she's married, right?"

"I suppose we can relax the rules a bit then." She entwined her fingers in his then squeezed his hand in a vice grip as Jana and Natalie skipped out together. "They're going to be sisters," she whispered, tears threatening to cascade again. And then a thought hit, and she turned to him, eyes wide. "Where are we going to live?"

"One thing at a time, my sweet. Let's get through this, and then we can start making plans."

The back door opened, and the girls climbed in, both jabbering at once. "This is funny," Jana said, looking from Amy to Miles and back again. "It's like we're a real—"

She was interrupted by Colton, opening the door on the other side. "Girls there." He pointed to the rear seat. "Cool kids in the middle."

Jana smacked him playfully on the arm. *Like brother and sister.* Amy knew exactly what Jana had been about to say. *It's like we're a real family.*

Miles drove to his house and parked in the driveway. The girls still jabbered, but Amy caught a look of confusion on Matt's face. Though the kids had been here more than she had, being here all together on a weekday afternoon was unusual.

As they trooped into the house, Miles said, "Before you run off and play, have a seat in the family room." Matt and Colton exchanged looks. Jana and Natalie simply followed orders. As the kids settled on the leather sectional facing the brick fireplace, Amy and Miles stepped in front of the hearth.

"Wait!" Matt clapped his hands. "You found treasure, right?"

Amy locked eyes with Miles. "As a matter of fact, we did."

"The best kind." Miles grasped her hand. "But before we show it to you, we have a couple of questions." With that, they both got down on one knee. Miles went first. "Matt, and Jana, would you make me the happiest man in the world and give me permission to—"

"Yes!" Colton jumped up and high-fived Matt. "I told you, bro!"

Matt slapped his hand again. "Like bro for real now."

"Wait." Jana's curls bounced as she looked at Amy and then Matt. "Are you…are you guys getting married?"

Natalie squealed.

Throat tight with emotion, Amy couldn't squeeze out another yes. But she didn't need to. In the next moment, they were mobbed by four cheering kids. When they finally extricated themselves, her cheeks were damp with tears. Leaning on Miles's shoulder, she simply listened as the girls chattered about what color they'd paint their room, wherever it was going to be, and the boys argued about whether they'd be Andersons or Allens or Anderson-Allens or Allen-Andersons. Looking up at Miles, she whispered, "This is going to get complicated, isn't it?"

"One thing at a time, my sweet. One thing at a time."

By one o'clock on Thanksgiving Day, Jeff and Tracy's house was filled with people and laughter and wonderful smells. A hand-lettered banner hung across the archway to the library.

Congratulations, Miles, Amy, Colton, Matt, Natalie, and Jana!

When Tracy said the word, they all gathered around the Eastlake table that had been at the center of family gatherings since the turn of the twentieth century.

Amy counted the crew. Twenty of Grandma Pearl's descendants, their spouses and adopted great-grands, plus Miles, Colton, Natalie, Brooke, Gavin, Niesha, and her fiancé, Emmett. Twenty-seven people bowed their heads as Jeff offered a blessing, and then they began passing platters around three tables. As Amy shuttled dishes between the table in the kitchen and the two set up in the library, she watched faces. Brooke and Gavin, who had been homeless this time last year but today would celebrate with this family that had welcomed them with open arms and then again tonight with the family they now had at Pop's Place. Niesha, who was only two days away from establishing her own home and family traditions. Colton and Natalie, whose homelife had been upended four years ago when their mother left, relinquished her parental rights, remarried, and moved to Paris. And Miles. Her fiancé. She had to pinch herself to believe it was real. He caught her staring and shot her a conspiratorial smile. The man was about to burst with the effort of keeping a secret from this gathering of family that would soon be his.

And finally, Matt and Jana, celebrating their third Thanksgiving here. Though it was clear they now felt they belonged, Amy still caught a glimpse of wonder in their eyes as they filled plates and laughed with cousins and friends. And soon-to-be siblings.

Thank You, Lord. Amy thought the words over and over as she refilled platters and bowls with turkey, mashed potatoes, gravy, stuffing, green bean casserole, sweet potatoes, and Grandma Pearl's squash rolls and "secret ingredient" cranberry sauce that called for dried tart cherries, cinnamon, and maple syrup.

When she and Tracy were finally able to sit at the table designated for the two older of the four generations present, the questions began. "I know some of the women heard this last night, but you have to fill the rest of us in. Start from yesterday morning and catch us up," Jeff said. "Spare no details."

For the next fifteen minutes, she and Miles told about their island adventure. He turned it over to Amy when they got to the part where she'd thought he was about to expire before her eyes and then proposed. When the laughter died, they told about their visit with Don Kennedy.

"So, the mystery is solved," Terry said.

"Most of it is." Miles pressed his shoulder against Amy's. "We still don't know where the real map is, and if there really was buried treasure or if we just happened to find someone's lost coin purse."

At that moment, Matt and Colton appeared in the doorway, empty plates in hand, in search of more potatoes and gravy.

"When are you going to take us to the island to search for more?" Matt asked.

Colton nodded. "Now it's our turn. We need to strategically divide up the whole island into grids like they did on Oak Island."

"Strategically, huh?" Miles laughed. "Maybe what we need to do is take the winter to make a strategic plan that we can carry out when the weather gets warmer."

Colton groaned, but Matt nudged him with his elbow. "That's actually a really cool plan. We can read up on Sea Dog Sam and study pirate activity in the area. It'll be fun."

"I guess." Colton didn't seem convinced.

Amy took their plates and filled them from the dishes on the table. As the two walked back into the library, they were already talking about making plans "like on Oak Island."

Miles laughed. "Like I said, there are still a lot of unanswered questions."

"We still don't know how and why *River Dancer* was trashed," Amy said. "Was it an accident, or done deliberately? And did Damon Kennedy ever serve time for stealing it and abducting Violet?"

"I wonder if she ever felt safe again," Aunt Ruth said.

That thought sobered everyone at the table until Tracy said, "The one thing we haven't done yet is find Grandma's diary from 1955. I've hunted, but there are still a ton of boxes we can look through."

Aunt Abigail nodded. "And probably some hiding places in the floors or walls that still haven't been discovered. I remember Dad saying, 'This house doesn't give up her secrets without a struggle.'"

"Searching for the diary sounds like a good thing to do while we're making room for pie," Aunt Ruth said.

Jeff shook his head. "You ladies have at it. The men have a Thanksgiving tradition we cannot break."

The women laughed. Miles looked from Jeff to Terry and then to Uncle Marvin. "I'm hoping that tradition involves snoring."

"Loudly," Jeff said. "You in?"

"Absolutely."

Chapter Twenty-Three

While naps commenced in the living room and the kids found games to play in the library and Sara and Anna settled their little ones for naps, the rest of the women headed up to the attic. This time they had seven pairs of hands. While Tracy gave instructions, telling Brooke and Niesha what piles had been sorted, Aunt Abigail's words tickled the back of Amy's mind. *This house doesn't give up her secrets easily.*

Were they looking in the wrong place? Grandma Pearl had written in diaries almost every day of her life. She'd probably written a detailed account of the disappearance of Violet and *River Dancer*. But if she'd been threatened, or felt Violet could still be in danger, she wouldn't have wanted anyone to find out what she knew. Amy stared up at the rafters, thinking how she'd almost missed finding the cigar box on the island. *If I were Grandma Pearl, where would I hide something I wanted to keep but didn't want anyone to find?*

They'd found several of her diaries from the 1930s hidden in a secret stairway. Didn't it make sense that she would have looked for a similar hiding place twenty years later? But where? Jeff had knocked out some walls as they remodeled, but there could still be cubby holes or trap doors they hadn't yet discovered.

"Over here!" Aunt Abigail yelled. As the others gathered around her, she pushed aside a large, flattened cardboard box that was leaning against a shelf. Behind it were six boxes, each marked with a *V*.

The younger women stood back while Aunt Ruth and Aunt Abigail opened the boxes and pulled out blouses, skirts, shoes, and jewelry, exclaiming, "Remember this?" and "She wore this when she took us to the fair." The last one was filled with notebooks, letters, a mirror and brush set, and a makeup bag containing the dried remains of Coty, Max Factor, and Maybelline cosmetics.

Amy reached for the notebooks, hoping to find something personal, but they were all college-ruled composition books filled with class notes and the occasional drawing of a flower or scrawls of *Mrs. Leonard Therwood*, or *Violet Therwood*.

"Whitney would go nuts over these clothes," Brooke said. "I suppose you have to give them back to Violet though."

While they wondered aloud what Violet's reaction would be to seeing her old belongings again, Niesha quietly stepped over to a full-length mirror, holding a gold, cinch-waisted dress to her chest.

Aunt Ruth let out a little gasp. "That was her going-away dress."

"What's that?" Niesha asked.

Aunt Ruth explained the once common tradition of a bride having a special outfit to wear when she left the church for her honeymoon.

The gold couldn't have been a more perfect complement to Niesha's bronze complexion. "That would fit you like a glove. Just like her wedding dress." Amy took out her phone and snapped a picture. "We need to get that cleaned. Tomorrow." When Niesha gave her a quizzical look, Amy said, "That's *your* going-away dress now, if you want it."

Niesha blinked back tears. "I wish... Do you think Violet could come to my wedding? Or would that be a bad idea? Would it make her feel bad, or would it be kind of like...closure?"

Amy put her arm around Niesha. "I think we should invite her and let her decide for herself."

When Jeff poked his head through the door and asked what time pie was going to be served, they put everything back in the boxes and headed to the kitchen. Amy was the last one down, and she took one final look around, wishing something would jump out at her. Grandma's diary from 1955 had to be somewhere in this house.

While Tracy and Robin cut pumpkin, pecan, and chocolate pies, Brooke and Niesha arranged dessert plates, coffee cups, and forks on the island. Amy took the chilled metal bowl out of the refrigerator and beat a quart of cream until peaks formed then stirred in powdered sugar, vanilla, and a dash of cinnamon.

Tracy had cut small enough pieces that anyone who wanted to could sample all three pies. They were hoping to have leftovers for tomorrow, but when a fourteen-year-old and two eleven-year-old boys ogled the desserts, Amy wasn't sure there'd be a forkful left. She laughed at Matt's incredulous expression when she told him he could have three pieces of the chocolate pie if he wanted, as long as he ate them one at a time.

When everyone was full once again, Amy gave Miles the "It's time" signal. He put on his jacket and quietly slipped out the back door. On cue, Jeff announced that he wanted everyone to gather in the living room for a Thanksgiving Day history lesson.

Kai and Matt groaned. Jana and Natalie mirrored each other's wrinkled-nose expressions. Amy ducked into the pantry and retrieved the sign she'd made late the night before. She and Miles might regret their decision in weeks to come, but today they would put smiles on their children's faces.

The commotion of bringing folding chairs into the living room and everyone finding seats had just settled when Miles returned. Amy met him at the back door. "I'll walk in first," she whispered. Then she reached around the box he carried and planted a kiss on his cheek. "You're wonderful."

"So are you. And a little bit crazy. It's not too late to change our minds, you know. About this. Or all of it."

"Oh yes it is. Sometimes you just have to jump in with both feet and deal with buyer's remorse later."

"I'm writing that into my vows. 'I promise to make it my life goal to never give you buyer's remorse.'"

She laughed and walked into the living room, holding up the sign that read HAPPY NATIONAL ADOPTION DAY, MATT & JANA. Her original plan, two days ago, was to stop there and let Miles take over. But yesterday had changed those plans. And the rest of their lives. She cleared her throat. "Today we celebrate Matt and Jana being adopted into this big, messy, noisy family, but it's our prayer that next Thanksgiving we'll be celebrating four more adoptions." She looked at Colton, who grinned back and gave a thumbs-up, then Matt, who copied the gesture. She turned to the girls, who unexpectedly rushed at her, one hugging each side. "So our gift is for all four of you." Without another word, she stepped aside, and Miles set the box in front of them.

The box jiggled, and Natalie shrieked. Jana gasped. "Is it? Is it?"

Colton pulled back the flaps on the box, and Matt let out a loud whoop and then bent and scooped up a wriggly black, white, and brown puppy with long, floppy ears.

"Meet Scrappy," Amy said over the chorus that filled the room. "He's a cavajack. A Cavalier King Charles spaniel and Jack Russell terrier mix."

"He's so, so, so cute." Jana's eyes glistened. "Thank you. Thank you. Thank you."

"Where's he going to live?" Natalie looked up at her father. "Can we keep him?"

"But I want—"

Miles held up a hand, interrupting Jana. "Shared custody. He'll spend equal time at each house until..." He put his arm around Amy and pulled her close. "Until we're all living under the same roof."

"We'll do all the work," Matt said.

"Yeah," Colton agreed. "The grownups won't have to do a thing."

Miles and Amy joined every other adult in the room in shared laughter and knowing looks.

After several minutes, Jeff interrupted the puppy talk. "Now it's time for the history lesson. I know I can't compete with all that cuteness, but listen up, kids. This is important." He ignored the reprise of groans. "We've all seen pictures of the Pilgrims. Men in their shiny buckled shoes, women with pretty lace caps. Just a bunch of nice people who wanted to worship God their way, so they got on a boat and sailed across the ocean to find a new home. I'm going to tell you the real account of what the pilgrims faced, based on accounts written in William Bradford's journal. Bradford was governor..."

Journal. Amy tiptoed around the perimeter of the room until she reached the aunts. Bending low, she whispered, "Did Violet keep a journal?"

Aunt Ruth nodded. "Yes. She kept it"—excitement danced in her eyes—"under the window seat in her room."

"We saw her put it in there a couple of times," Aunt Abigail whispered, "but when we went looking for it, we could never find it. I wonder…"

"Tell Tracy," Amy whispered. Without another word, she turned and hurried into the foyer and up the stairs to the room with the bow window over a cushioned window seat.

A window seat that opened.

But it couldn't be in there. She'd seen the top up when Jeff was remodeling. It was empty at the time. And she'd hidden in it as a child. It was the best place to hide in the whole house.

Her excitement fading, she dropped to her knees, tossed throw pillows onto the floor, and opened the window seat. Blankets. The window seat was full of blankets. With a sigh, she brought the seat down again, hearing the familiar whine of the hinges. She was about to get up when something stopped her. A feeling in the pit of her stomach.

It made no logical sense, but she started pulling blankets out, one at a time, until the box was empty. Nothing but dark-stained wood.

Disappointment swelled, yet she still felt the nudge to not give up. She took her phone out of her pocket and swept the light around the inside like she'd done in the cabin on the island. Nothing. She held her phone in one hand and trailed the other hand across the bottom and then around the sides. Was that a ridge? Or maybe a crack. Or just two boards that had slightly separated with age? When she followed the line with her fingers, she traced a square. She ducked her head into the opening, turning until she was practically upside down. Tiny gold hinges were tucked under the rim of the window seat.

She felt around the square and found a barely perceptible indentation, just enough to stick her fingernails into. She lifted, and it sprang open. A small cubbyhole, completely hidden. Only large enough for two books.

She pulled them out. On the inside cover of one was an inscription.

> *December 25, 1954*
> *Merry Christmas and Happy 33rd Birthday to my much-loved wife.*
> *Howard*

Inside the next was written:

> *May 4, 1955*
> *Violet,*
> *"The LORD is nigh unto them that are of a broken heart; and saveth such as be of a contrite spirit." Psalm 34:18*
>   *With all our love,*
>   *Howard, Pearl, Abigail, Ruthy, and Noah*

July 21, 1955

Violet is safe! At least for now. Lenny came to the house late last night. I was at a meeting at church. He told Howard that Violet is fine. They are married and have changed their name. He refused to give any more details. He said we should stop trying to find her, because there are people who might hurt her, or us, because of what we know. Howard asked about the boat. Lenny doesn't know what happened to it, but he assured Howard that he and Violet were not responsible and that we should tell the police to stop looking. He didn't want to take any of Violet's things, because he was on foot—he'd parked a mile away in case someone had followed him, and snuck through yards to get here. I wish I'd been home. I would have given him Vi's diary. I don't know if her account would ever hold up in court, but I pray justice will someday be served. Don Kennedy needs to pay for what he did to her and what he took from us. Lenny left a letter from Violet. It made me feel so much better and yet so very sad.

I don't know what to tell the children. I don't think we can let them know about Lenny's visit. Children talk. It might be safest if we stick to saying we don't have all the answers. It's not a lie. Will our questions ever get answered?

Chapter Twenty-Four

The Allen women gathered around the dining table at nine the next morning. Black Friday shopping couldn't compete with Grandma Pearl and Violet's diaries from the summer of 1955. They took turns reading out loud. After an hour, they'd read all of Violet's entries, which stopped the night before she disappeared, and Grandma Pearl's through the end of July.

Amy pulled pen and paper from her purse and began writing down what they knew. "Grandma Pearl knew Violet was okay, but still in danger. She thought Don was the one who abducted her. Up to this point, the only time she mentioned Damon was in April when she said he had come for dinner with the college kids and Damon seemed 'like a very disturbed young man.'"

Aunt Ruth nodded. "She didn't know what happened to *River Dancer*. Unless we learn more later in her diary, or from Don or Violet, we may never find out how it ended up in pieces and partially burned and buried."

"We still don't know how, or if, Professor Janvier was involved," Aunt Abigail added.

Amy began turning pages in Grandma Pearl's diary, searching for familiar names. She stopped suddenly when a name jumped off the page. "Look at this." She began reading out loud.

September 10, 1955. The strangest thing happened today. I'm going to try to record it word for word, exactly as it happened, in case we are someday asked to give testimony in court.

Howard got a call from Antoine Janvier, asking if he could come to our house around four. When he got here, he looked distraught. Unshaven, tie askew, very unlike the always impeccably dressed Frenchman. We sat down to coffee and chatted a bit, then all of a sudden he pulled a check out of his pocket and slid it across the table. The check was for a thousand dollars!

"I learned that my nephew was involved in the theft of your boat and Violet Conway's disappearance," he said. "This news came out of a therapy session at the institution where he is currently residing. Though it may cost me my marriage, I have reported this to the police, and I want to make things right with you."

To say we were stunned was an understatement. I think I stuttered when I said, "Your nephew?"

Antoine seemed about to break down as he said, "Damon Kennedy. Sally is his aunt. And Don's, though Damon has always been her favorite. She has protected him from consequences his whole life so that he has never learned to exercise self-control or take responsibility for his own actions." The poor man put his head in his hands and looked absolutely miserable.

"Damon was working with Don?" Howard asked.

"No," he said. "Don was trying to protect Violet from Damon."

When we both expressed confusion, he explained that Damon had been down on his luck, over his head in debt. He assumed Don told Damon about the map. Somehow, Don got Violet out of the house and took the boat keys. Why, oh why, didn't we hear anything? While they were anchored by Hogback Island, ready to search for the treasure, Don told Violet to jump overboard and then knocked Damon out.

Amy looked up. "The X was on Teal Island, not Hogback."
Tracy leaned forward. "Keep reading!"
"Yes, ma'am!"

"After he came to, Damon headed south where no one would recognize him. He was going way too fast and hit a rock. River Dancer was damaged beyond repair, so he set it on fire and sank it. But before he did that, he cut off as much of the name board as he could and buried that and Violet's purse on the shore. He's the one who sent the dolls and the warnings while he hid out in Crystal City. He became extremely paranoid, sure that someone was going to turn him in or the men he owed money to would find him. Eventually, he admitted himself to the St. Louis County Lunatic Asylum."

Amy checked on the turkey casserole in the oven and declared it needed just a few more minutes. Jeff, Terry, and Uncle Marvin had taken the kids to a movie and out for lunch so there wouldn't be any distractions during their time with Violet and Don. They'd be home around one thirty, and Miles, his children, the Pasternaks, and Maura Childs would be joining them.

She'd called Don and Abby Ruth yesterday to make sure the added company wouldn't be overwhelming. Both had said they wanted anyone who had been affected by their story to be present. Now Amy glanced at the clock, nervous about how the next few hours would play out. "Should we ask questions, or just let things happen?"

"Let's be ready to facilitate or intervene if necessary," Aunt Abigail said. "This is more about them than us. Does Violet know Don is going to be here?"

Amy wiped her damp hands on her pants. "I don't know. I left that up to her daughter."

Tracy paced in front of the window that faced the driveway. "I told both of them to pull up to the garage and use the back door." The sound of a car made her jump. "Don and Muriel are here."

Aunt Ruth twisted the bottom of her apron then put her hand on her sister's shoulder. "I can't believe we actually get to see Violet after all these years. I don't know if I'm ready to see her in her eighties."

"Or to have her see us." Aunt Abigail winked. "We used to be cute."

Tracy opened the back door and held out a hand to Muriel. Don followed, walking with a steady gate that belied his age. Amy ushered them to the table. They'd labored over the seating arrangement, deciding to put Don at the end closest to the door, with Muriel to his right and Violet to his left. Amy pulled out a chair for Muriel but addressed a comment to Don. "We've all been praying for this to go smoothly."

"So have we." Don sat and then ran slightly trembling fingers across the edge of the table. "Was this your grandparents'?"

"Yes."

"It was right here, at this table, that I first heard the Gospel," he said. "Your grandmother was wearing a new dress, and your grandfather jokingly called her his Pearl of great price."

Amy smiled. "And that launched her into a sermon, I bet."

"Yep." He closed his eyes. "Mind you, I had no interest in it at the time, but out on that island, all alone, her words came back to me. I memorized the verse soon after I left the island. 'The kingdom of heaven is like unto a merchant man seeking goodly pearls: who, when he had found one pearl of great price, went and sold all that he had, and bought it.'" His eyes glistened when he opened them. "She went on to explain that knowing Jesus was worth more than anything else we would ever own or strive after, and then she recited the verse about storing up treasure in heaven. That was long before Vi found the map, but it seemed prophetic when I was on the island searching for treasure to no avail. I realized that even if I'd found a chest full of gold, there would still be this emptiness in my soul." He patted his chest. "I didn't know much about God, but out there, all alone, I told Him I needed Him."

"And he hasn't looked back since," Muriel said, patting his arm.

Tracy went to the door again. Amy glanced out the window. The white Tesla hadn't made a sound. As a woman Amy guessed must be Abby Ruth walked around to the passenger door and helped an elderly woman out, Aunt Ruth released a gasp. "It's her," she whispered.

The two visitors stepped into the enclosed back porch, and Amy was shocked to see a woman who could have been a movie actress. Beautifully coiffed silvery hair, tasteful makeup that accented high cheekbones and sparkling, bright eyes. Her face was lined, but in a way that showed joy rather than age. She moved with poise and grace as her daughter helped her off with her coat. She wore a white wool blazer over a navy collarless blouse accented with a blue and white scarf and a string of pearls that matched her earrings.

Don stood as she walked through the door. Violet didn't seem to notice him as Aunt Ruth and Aunt Abigail stepped in front of her and started to introduce themselves.

"No introductions necessary." Violet stretched out her arms. "I would know my girls anywhere."

The reunion brought tears to Amy's eyes. So many years, so many questions, would all be put to rest today. When the little huddle separated, Tracy held out a box of tissues and introduced herself, Amy, and Robin. Before she had a chance to say more, Don walked around his wife and stopped three feet from Violet. "Vi." His voice was just above a whisper.

Violet stared for a moment, confusion dimming her smile. And then, shock. "Don?" The tone of her voice matched his.

Amy held her breath, sure she wasn't the only one in the room watching in nervous suspense.

Don nodded. Violet reached out to steady herself on a chair. "Before…before we talk about anything, I need to know something. Were you…protecting me, or…"

"Yes. I would never have done anything to hurt you. Damon threatened to—"

Violet held up a perfectly manicured hand to stop him. "That's all I need to know right now. Let's enjoy the meal these precious women have prepared and catch up on the past decades, and then we can talk about those things." She reached out and hugged him. "So good to see you. Now introduce me to your lovely wife."

Chapter Twenty-Five

After Tracy asked the blessing, Amy noticed Violet doing the exact same thing Don had done, running a fingertip along the edge of the table in front of her. Only she seemed to be searching for something. After a moment, she stopped. "Feel this," she said to Aunt Abigail, pointing to a half-moon-shaped scar. "You put this here with your toy flour sifter. You got mad at me when I said we couldn't eat the cookies we'd made until after supper, and you slammed that little aluminum thing down on the table." She smiled. "I'm so glad no one removed it. I'm a firm believer in not hiding our scars. They make us who we are." She turned to Don, layers of meaning in her warm expression.

As they passed around the turkey and stuffing casserole, cranberry Jell-O salad, and rolls, Violet suggested they take turns sharing highlights from the years they'd been separated. So they talked of weddings and births and jobs and grandchildren. Violet got misty-eyed when she told about Lenny's battle with cancer. She patted Abby Ruth's hand. "Until his last breath, he honored God with his whole heart and loved us well."

Once again, Amy watched Don for a reaction. The briefest of shadows seemed to cross his face before he gave a slight nod. Muriel reached for his hand resting on the table, and squeezed it. Did she know her husband had once had a crush on Violet? By the look on her face, Amy guessed she did, and that it didn't matter.

Violet's caramel apple buckle was even better than Aunt Ruth had described it. Rich and gooey, with a hint of heat Amy couldn't identify, and topped with whipped cream "with a touch of cinnamon, just the way Pearl taught me," it was a hit with everyone. After a few bites, Aunt Ruth said, "You promised to give us your secret."

After dabbing her mouth with her napkin, Violet smiled. "I did. I believe I promised to tell you everything you wanted to know." She picked up her fork and scooped up a bite of buckle. "The secret ingredient is mace. And you"—she nodded at Aunt Ruth—"actually get the credit for it. The first time I made it here, you were helping me. You were so proud that you could reach the cinnamon at the back of the spice drawer and measure it yourself. Just before we mixed it, I saw the label on the bottle." Violet laughed. "I scooped out all I could, but there was enough left to give it a little bit of a kick. I've been adding it ever since. Thank you, my dear."

"It's delicious, Vi," Don said. "I remember you serving it when all of us were together. You and Lenny, Sil and Rina, Howard and Pearl, and the three little ones. 'Bittersweet' is a word I use more and more as time marches on."

They sat in silence for the next few minutes. Amy watched the clock, the minute hand ticking toward the six. The porch door squeaked open, and Miles and the kids came in. When the moviegoers came home, a whirlwind of introductions and who-belongs-to-who ensued. The kids took over the library, and the adults moved to the living room. After they'd settled and Jeff had taken orders for coffee and tea, the Pasternaks arrived. Tracy led them in, and Amy watched with tears in her eyes as friends who had been separated by decades, distrust, and unanswered questions were reunited.

The aunts had carefully thought out the seating arrangement here too, putting Violet, Don and Muriel, and Silas and Katerina close together. "The rest of us are just here to listen," Aunt Abigail had said. She glanced at Amy. "Except when it comes to adding the things you've learned that Vi and Don probably don't know."

Amy looked at the time on her phone. Where was Maura? They'd offered to pick her up, assuming she no longer drove, but she'd said she could get there on her own.

After a few minutes of catching up, Violet said, "I suppose we should start with the map."

At that moment, Amy's phone, sitting on the arm of her chair, began to vibrate. "It's Maura." She stood and walked into the foyer before saying hello.

"I'm on my way." The little woman sounded breathless. "I'm bringing some of William's things for Violet. I still can't believe I'm going to see her again. Can someone run out and help me with these boxes? I'm only bringing two. Just the things I thought would be most important to her. And one thing I have no clue about."

Amy wanted to ask her to clarify, but simply told her to honk when she parked in front of the house and a couple of the men would come out and help her.

When she returned, Kai, Matt, and Colton stood in the doorway. She motioned for them to come in and sit on the floor and then tuned in to Violet's story in progress.

"In a desk drawer in my father's home office, I found something flat and wrapped in cloth. It was a map. A very, very old map drawn on some kind of animal skin. At first, I didn't recognize anything on it, but 'Mississippi River' was spelled out in a curved line, following the bends of the river as it flowed around four islands. The islands were numbered, and there was an X in the middle of one. I showed it to Pearl and then to several friends. It was Don who recognized the islands. They'd changed in shape over the years, but we were sure the map showed the islands we now know as Willow, Hogback, and Teal. The smallest one, which we found out had once been called Diamond Island, no longer existed. We took the map to Professor Janvier, a history professor who had been my father's closest friend. He thought it appeared to be more than a hundred years old, which confirmed our suspicions, our hopes, that what I'd found was indeed a pirate treasure map." With these last words, Violet smiled at the three boys who sat cross-legged on the floor, hanging on every word.

"We made a pact," Don said, picking up the story. "We promised not to tell anyone about the map, and we started making plans to explore the islands together in search of the treasure." He looked down at his hands in his lap. When he looked up again, his eyes glistened. "I don't know if you can believe this, Vi, but I was not the one who broke that promise."

Surprise clearly registered on Violet's face. "Who…" A deep grove formed between her eyes. "Then how did Damon find out about it?"

"All along, I thought it was Ellen. I had broken off our relationship, and I assumed she was just getting back at me." His eyes seemed to plead with Violet. "Yesterday, we celebrated Thanksgiving with our children, grandchildren, and Damon's wife. They separated years ago because of his erratic behavior, but we have always remained close to her. When I told her I was going to meet you today, and how hard it would be because everyone assumed I had told Damon about the map, she told us what really happened." He sighed. "When we went to Professor Janvier's house to show him the map, his wife, Sally, was eavesdropping. And she knew Damon had a ten-thousand-dollar gambling debt."

Violet covered her mouth.

Don turned away and met the gazes of the rest of their audience. "Damon and I have the same father, but different mothers. Professor Janvier's wife was our aunt. She was best friends with Damon's mother. Even before our father's indiscretion became public, Sally Janvier hated my very existence."

"And mine." Violet frowned. "I worked a few afternoons a week in the bursar's office. Mrs. Janvier also worked there. When some numbers weren't making sense, I started inquiring. I never did find absolute proof, but I'm sure she was embezzling. I was Professor Janvier's assistant for one of his classes, and I talked to him about it. He, or someone, told her, and she came unglued. So angry. One night at a church function, Mrs. Janvier got so furious at me she left bruises on my arm. I was afraid of what else she might be capable of. The professor refused to report her, so I did. I never found out if anyone followed up on my claims." Violet looked at Don. "You mentioned Damon's erratic behavior. I have to wonder if that ran in the family."

As the missing story pieces fell into place, Amy watched Violet's countenance change. Was this the first time she'd told anyone other than Lenny her part of the story? A tear slipped down Violet's cheek. "When Sally overheard us talking about the map, she must have thought it would give her a way to help Damon and hurt me at the same time." She turned to Don. "I thought, hoped, you were trying to save me, but I thought it was only because you felt guilty for telling him—"

Don shook his head. "I would never…" He pressed his lips together.

"I'm so sorry I doubted you." Violet's voice was low and hoarse. "I should have known."

Don waved a hand in a gesture that said he understood. "No one knew Damon was mentally ill. We just tried to find ways to appease him when he was in one of his moods. When I told him I wouldn't allow him to steal the map, he flew into a rage. It was the only time he'd ever attacked me physically, but it terrified me. I should have called the police. That is my biggest regret."

He took a moment to steady his voice. "I'm so sorry. For everything. For terrifying you and for you feeling you couldn't come back here. And I'm sorry for all of us not having a chance to search for the treasure. I spent a couple of weeks on that island and never found anything, but I'd only seen the map that once and couldn't be sure I was looking in the right cove. I promise you, it all would have been yours if I'd found it. Damon never showed up during that time. I have no idea if that map ever led him to—" Don stopped talking when Violet began laughing.

Amy stared at her. Was she having some kind of breakdown? After a moment, Violet shook her head. "After you warned me, I stayed up all night, soaking a piece of leather I cut from an old purse in strong tea then drying it under my hair dryer." She smiled at the stunned look on Don's face. "The map I gave Damon was a fake."

Chapter Twenty-Six

Abby Ruth hovered next to Violet as they walked up the stairs to her old room, but it didn't look to Amy like Violet needed any assistance. She stopped at the bedroom door then took several slow steps toward the window.

"I was sitting at my desk. It was still dark out, about four in the morning, I think. I'd hidden the real map and was examining the one I'd made, when something shattered the glass and clanged onto the floor. I never found what it was, but a note fluttered to the floor. It said—"

"'Bring the map, get the boat keys, come out the back door. If you don't, I'll break in.'" Don stood in the doorway. "Damon wrote it, but he twisted it around my class ring so you'd think it was from me."

"I never found the ring. You were both waiting for me. Even though you'd told me to escape, I thought you were both..." Violet looked as though she didn't have the energy, or maybe just the desire, to finish the sentence. She turned away from Don and walked to the window seat.

"Amy already found your diary in there," Tracy said. "And Grandma Pearl's from 1955. There's nothing else in there."

Violet nodded yet turned back to the window seat and opened the lid. She reached inside and ran her fingers along the edge on the opposite side from where Amy had found the hidden compartment. She slid her fingernails into an almost invisible groove, and a small door opened. "It's still here." She held up what looked like a rolled scroll tied with a leather string.

The real treasure map.

Violet clutched it to her chest and smiled at Don. "I suppose they'll say we're too old for that expedition."

Don laughed. "I, for one, never listen to what 'they' say."

"Good." She pointed beyond him with the map. "Let's go down and join Sil and Rina. We'll all look at it together. Just like the first time."

Back in the living room, Amy and Tracy cleared the cups from the coffee table while the old friends settled in their seats. The boys, who'd been sitting on the outside of the circle, stood to get a better view. Violet untied the cord then set the map on the table and slowly unrolled it. Unlike the pencil sketch Amy and Miles had found at the college, the islands were not labeled on this one. Don leaned down and pointed to the *X* on Teal Island. "That's farther north than I thought. I didn't get that far." His eyes lit as he looked up. "I bet it's still there."

"We'll go!" Matt said. "We'll search for you. Colton's dad has a boat. I wouldn't even care if I couldn't keep any of it. I just want to find real buried treasure."

Violet smiled. "I suppose we should let the younger generations do the work for us. I accept your offer, sir." She winked at Amy. "If your parents agree, of course."

Matt and Colton's high five reverberated off the fireplace just as a car horn beeped outside. Jeff and Terry went out to help Maura with the boxes. Maura walked in ahead of them, and Violet was on her feet and walking toward her in seconds. The two hugged and cried and hugged some more. When they finally pulled apart, Maura pointed at the boxes the men had set on the floor. A name plate with PROFESSOR WILLIAM CONWAY sat on top of one. Among other things, the box contained framed photographs, a small globe, and a bust of D. Pat Henderson, one of the founders of Culver-Stockton College. A metal box sat atop a stack of file folders on the other.

Violet bent and picked up the box. About a foot square and four inches high, the box had a handle on top and was painted black and dented in several places. As Violet lifted it, several things rolled around inside. "It looks like a cash box." She tried to open it. "It's locked."

Amy took a step closer. On the front of the box was a small keyhole. She didn't quite suppress a gasp before turning on her heel and calling, "Just a minute," over her shoulder. Almost running, she spun around the corner into the kitchen, whipped open the pantry door, and grabbed her purse from the counter. As she hurried back to the living room, she opened the zipper pocket on the inside, pulled out the only thing it contained, and handed it to Violet. "We found this in your purse."

"My purse? You mean the one I had on the boat? Was it in the box with the dolls?"

"No. It was under a tree in the river." When Violet's eyebrows disappeared under feathered silver bangs, Amy put a hand on her arm. "We'll tell you all about that later."

Violet nodded slowly and turned her attention back to the key. She stared at it, at first with a blank look, and then her eyes suddenly widened. "The mortician gave this to me. It was in my father's vest pocket when he died." She seemed to sway slightly, and Amy suggested they sit down at the table so everyone could see the metal box. In reality, she was afraid Violet might faint.

Everyone sat on the edge of their chairs as Violet brought the key to the keyhole. She sucked in a breath and didn't release it. The key slid in. She turned it to the right, and they heard a click.

The hinges protested with a loud squeak as Violet lifted the lid. The cover opened all the way, resting against the table. An envelope addressed to William Conway sat on top. Violet nudged it aside and picked up a small metal object. It was only when she held it out in the palm of her hand that Amy could identify it. A curved sword, less than two inches long, with a basket guard around the hilt.

"A cutlass!" Matt exclaimed. "A pirate cutlass!"

Violet reached back in the box and picked up another piece. This time, Don was the one to identify it. "That's a percussion pistol. What in the world?"

"Pirates used those!" This came from Jana. Amy hadn't even seen her and Natalie enter the room.

"Maybe," Violet said, voice just above a whisper. She took the letter out, exposing the entire contents of the metal box. Four more small metal pieces. A treasure chest, a gold coin, a coiled rope, and a flag bearing a skull and crossbones.

"That's the Jolly Roger!" Colton yelled.

"I bet these were clues for the treasure," Matt said.

"Maybe pirates traded them, like money," Miles added.

As guesses began to volley across the room, Violet picked up the envelope and pulled out a single sheet of paper. As she read silently, her lips parted. She covered her mouth with her hand. Her shoulders began to shake. Amy thought she was crying until she noticed the crinkles at the corners of Violet's eyes. Eyes that shone with mirth. After several seconds, she lowered her hand, let out a beautiful laugh, and laid the letter on the table for everyone to read.

> The Palmer Company
> 124 28th Street
> New York, New York
>
> April 2, 1955
> Dear Dr. Conway,
> Thank you for your submission to The Palmer Company. Our acquisitions team is delighted to inform you that we wish to purchase your exciting new board game, Mississippi Gold. Our research and development team is already hard at work to find ways to mass produce authentic-looking maps like the one you sent.
> We were all entertained by the backstory about Sea Dog Sam and have sent your query letter on to our book publishing division. We believe there is great potential for a book to accompany the unique treasure hunt board game you've created...

Niesha paced from one end of the Captain's Table banquet room to the other. Every time she reached the long, opaque white garment bag hanging from a hook on the back of the door, she stopped, closed her eyes, whispered to herself, and moved on. As she paced, Amy, Tracy, and Robin tried to reassure her that everything was going to be just fine.

The wedding rehearsal was scheduled to start in half an hour, but there was someone Niesha had asked to meet first.

Amy ducked her head out of the room for about the tenth time, surveying the empty River Dan's dining room. A shaft of light poked into the room as the front door opened. Aunt Abigail, Aunt Ruth, Abby Ruth, and Violet stepped in, stopping under the sign over the back door. Amy had glanced up at it as she'd rushed in with two garment bags over her arm and a nervous Niesha at her side. It looked shinier and less worn in the morning light.

Batting away all of the what-ifs assaulting her peace, Amy waved to them, motioning for the women to come into the banquet room. When they'd joined her and removed their coats, she made introductions. Violet and Abby Ruth had spent the rest of the afternoon at Aunt Ruth's house, and all four women had taken naps, so Violet looked refreshed and bright-eyed, in spite of hours of talking and all the revelations that must be taking an emotional toll. When introduced to Niesha, she said, "Amy tells me you have a story to share with me."

Amy suggested they sit in the chairs she'd placed in a semi-circle in front of the fireplace where a fire softly crackled. Niesha kept standing, hands behind her back. She faced Violet. "I'm so thrilled to meet you. This might sound silly, but when Amy told me about you, when I heard how you'd lost your father and the Allen family took you in, it made me feel like we were kindred spirits. When I first met Amy, I was scared and alone. I grew up in the foster system, never feeling wanted, but then her entire family welcomed me, and for the first time I feel like I belong." She shook out a tissue and blew her nose before continuing.

"When I got engaged, I assumed Emmett and I would get married at the courthouse with just a few friends, but then these amazing women offered their help." Niesha smiled. "I'd never been the little girl who lay in bed imagining a long white dress or a tiered wedding cake and flowers. But then Amy encouraged me to dream big, and she gave me this book to look at." Niesha brought her hand from behind her back. She held out Violet's bride book, and Violet took it with shaky hands.

Tears slid down Violet's cheeks, making dark fuchsia dots on her pale pink blouse. Her voice shook as she laughed. "I always teased Pearl about never throwing anything away. I take it all back." She paged through the book, stopping at the dress pattern for her wedding gown and laying her hand over it. "Lenny and I had a beautiful little ceremony in his grandmother's backyard, but oh, how I grieved over this." She looked up. "Do you know if she kept it?" She addressed the question to Aunt Ruth, but it was Niesha who answered.

"She did." She stepped to the door and took the long white bag from behind it. Amy stood and unzipped the garment bag.

Violet gasped. As she reached out to touch a pearl, sobs shook her shoulders. Her daughter put her arms around her and offered her a tissue. The other women in the room waited in silence, all with tears in their eyes and all, Amy knew, praying for comfort.

After a moment, Violet looked up and stood. A smile began to slowly emerge, erasing her momentary sorrow like sunlight breaking through a cloud. "Does it fit you?"

Tears dripped from Niesha's lashes as she nodded. "Without a single alteration. But I have another dress, and I won't wear this if you—"

"Shh." Violet pressed one hand to Niesha's cheek. "I never told anyone, but as I sewed this, I prayed over it, not just for my marriage, but for the women who would wear it after me. This family taught me that God delights in giving second chances. Apparently, even for wedding gowns. Nothing would make me happier than to watch my kindred spirit walk down the aisle in this."

The Allen women and girls, plus Lisa and Violet, gathered in the bride's room on Saturday morning, forming a circle around Niesha, who was wearing the long gown studded with pearls. One by one, they took turns praying a blessing over her. Amy opened her eyes as Aunt Abigail prayed, imagining what it would feel like when she stood in the center of this circle of love.

After the final "Amen," a male voice called from outside the curtain. "May we come in?"

Aunt Ruth opened the partition. Dan and Josh Jordan walked in. Josh carried a long, flat, piece of wood. "I had a friend make a copy for us," Dan said.

"But this one belongs to all of you," Josh added. He turned the board faceup, and the women gathered around him.

Aunt Ruth, Aunt Abigail, and Violet reached out simultaneously to touch the names crudely carved under *River Dancer*.

Minutes later, Amy walked a beaming Niesha down the aisle, kissed her cheek, and took her place between Miles and Matt. Miles reached over and lifted her left hand, touched her ring, and then leaned close to her and whispered, "Some things gold can stay. Forever."

Amy squeezed his hand in response. As they watched their daughters, who were grinning from the front of the church and wearing dresses made sixty-eight years ago for two other little girls, she leaned into Miles and let herself dream of her own happily ever after. Looking up at her fiancé, her smile was meant only for him. Then she whispered the words Violet had said yesterday. "God delights in giving second chances." For friendships. And rings. And love.

Dear Reader,

When I started writing this part of Amy's story, I was remembering back to the days when my four sons were young and life was always crazy busy. Some of the busyness came from their involvement in church and school activities, but a lot of it came from my desire to make a difference, if not in the world, then at least in my community. I got in on the ground floor of a maternity home ministry, then took on the job of director of a crisis pregnancy center, then helped start a teen center for at-risk kids. In the midst of all that, I wrote and directed plays for our church, homeschooled a couple of our boys, and started to write fiction. Whew! I'm exhausted just thinking back on it! As I wrote about Amy's overcommitment, I tried to analyze my reasons for saying "Yes" to so many things. All good causes, definitely, but were my motives always totally altruistic? Probably not. It feels good to be needed, doesn't it? And sometimes, as young moms, we crave the appreciation of someone who isn't leaving Cheerios and Legos on our floor!

So here I am, twenty years older than Amy, with lots of hard-earned wisdom and advice for young mothers on finding balance, making time for God, family, serving, and self-care, but the irony is that, within months of signing a contract for *Nothing Gold Can Stay*, I found myself doing exactly what caused so much stress for my fictional friend. When offered another contract for a book with the same deadline, I cheerfully said yes, and then yes again. Could I speak at a women's conference? Of course! Take part in a prayer ministry? I would be honored. Host Melby Kid Kamp for nine grandkids? You betcha! And there I was, living out the scenario I was writing about.

So, my advice to overcommitted women of any age? Be gentle. Don't beat yourself up. Take one day, or one minute, at a time. Ask God to order your days. Divide your to-do lists into manageable chunks. Take breaks. Ask for help. Remember, peanut butter sandwiches can constitute a meal—no guilt. And next time a great opportunity comes along, think twice and pray before saying yes. Amy and I are rooting for you!

Blessings,
Becky Melby

About The Author

Becky Melby has authored twenty-two contemporary fiction titles, including seven, to date, for Guideposts cozy mystery series. Married to her high school sweetheart for fifty years, mother of four, grandmother to fifteen, Becky thrives on writing, reading, camping, riding on the back of a silver Gold Wing motorcycle, and time with family.

COLLECTIBLES from GRANDMA'S ATTIC

Could There Really Be Buried Pirate Treasure in the Upper Mississippi River Valley?

The hints of pirate treasure in *Nothing Gold Can Stay* aren't all fictional. According to *Geological Wonder and Curiosities of Missouri* by Thomas R. Beveridge, Blackbeard the Pirate may have buried his treasure in Jefferson County, Missouri, located just south of Saint Louis County.

Legend has it that exceptionally high waters during the rainy season permitted Blackbeard to sail up Joachim Creek and into the area that is now Harrison Lake. Receding water left his pirate vessel stranded, so he buried his loot near the natural bridge south of the present lake. The ship was then rolled on logs for four miles overland and launched into the Mississippi River near Crystal City, Missouri.

The Saint Louis area has other pirate legends too. John Baptiste Lafitte was famous for providing his band of pirates—one thousand strong—to General Jackson in the war of 1812. He disappeared around 1826, but a journal purportedly written by Lafitte surfaced in the 1950s. This journal says he eventually moved to Saint Louis, under the name John Lafflin, to raise a family. He died in the 1850s and is buried in the nearby Mississippi River town of Alton, Illinois.

Pirates were active on the Mississippi until the summer of 1803, when a detachment of US Cavalry was sent to camp at Devil's Bake Oven in Grand Tower, Illinois, an infamous pirate hideaway. They had orders to stay until they'd either wiped out the bad guys or driven them away. By the end of that summer, the troops had done exactly that.

But the question still remains… Did the pirates leave anything behind?

SOMETHING DELICIOUS From GRANDMA PEARL'S RECIPE BOX

Violet's Caramel Apple Skillet Buckle

Ingredients:

- ½ cup butter, softened
- ¾ cup sugar
- 2 large eggs, room temperature
- 1 teaspoon vanilla extract
- 2 cups all-purpose flour
- 2½ teaspoons baking powder
- 1¾ teaspoons ground cinnamon (Or, like Violet, substitute ¼ tsp. of mace for the same amount of cinnamon)
- ½ teaspoon ground ginger
- ¼ teaspoon salt
- 1½ cups buttermilk

Topping:

- ⅔ cup packed brown sugar
- ½ cup all-purpose flour
- ¼ cup cold butter
- ¾ cup finely chopped pecans
- ½ cup old-fashioned oats
- 6 cups thinly sliced peeled Gala or other sweet apples (about 6 medium)
- 18 caramels, unwrapped
- 1 tablespoon buttermilk
- Optional toppings: Vanilla ice cream, whipped cream, additional chopped pecans and ground cinnamon

Directions:

1. Preheat oven to 350 degrees. In large bowl, cream butter and sugar until light and fluffy, 5–7 minutes. Add eggs, one at a time, beating well after each addition. Beat in vanilla. In another bowl, whisk flour, baking powder, cinnamon, ginger, and salt; add to creamed mixture alternately with buttermilk, beating well after each addition. Pour into greased 12-inch cast-iron or other oven-proof skillet.
2. For topping, in small bowl, mix brown sugar and flour; cut in butter until crumbly. Stir in pecans and oats, sprinkle over batter. Top with apples. Bake until apples are golden brown, 60–70 minutes. Cool in pan on wire rack.
3. In microwave, melt caramels with buttermilk and stir until smooth. Drizzle over cake. Let stand until set. Serve with toppings as desired.

*Read on for a sneak peek of another exciting book
in the Secrets from Grandma's Attic series!*

The Cameo Clue

By Shirley Raye Redmond

Tracy Doyle ventured once again into Grandma Pearl's attic late Sunday afternoon—this time in search of potential props for the church's upcoming Christmas pageant—wondering if she would ever get everything done on her holiday to-do list.

"There's a cheap wooden jewelry box stashed away in a footlocker, as I recall," her aunt Ruth said as Tracy and her sister, Amy, made their way up the stairs. "You can spray-paint the box gold and add some glitter or fake gems. One of the wisemen can carry it. Of course, my memory isn't what it used to be. I may have already given that old box away. I'm not as young as I used to be, and neither is my mind. What do I know?"

Amy chuckled, whispering to Tracy, "I've heard that before."

Tracy laughed as she trudged up the narrow steps ahead of her sister. Aunt Ruth had stayed behind to help with dishes following the family's Sunday meal after church. Everyone else had gone home. Miles Anderson, Amy's fiancé, had taken Amy's kids, Matt and Jana, and his own two kids, Colton and Natalie, to the ice-skating rink for an afternoon of fresh air and exercise.

"The footlocker is a burgundy one with silver rivets," Aunt Ruth hollered after them. "Shouldn't be too hard to find."

"Oh, sure, easy for her to say," Amy grumbled, following close on Tracy's heels.

At the top of the stairs, Tracy stopped to catch her breath. She tugged the chain of the overhead light. Gesturing toward the crowded attic room, she declared, "One of these days we're going to have everything up here totally organized."

Amy laughed. "So you keep saying. But we are making progress." She indicated the folding tables and neat piles of items that had already been sorted.

"I mean it this time. We've still got to weed out more stuff." Collectibles were one thing. Junk was another. Tracy glanced around the room, hoping to catch sight of a burgundy footlocker. It was chilly in the attic, but not too cold. The December weather had been warmer than usual. Amy's kids had been praying for snow. Truth be told, most of the kids in Canton were probably praying for snow too.

Amy stepped around her, nearly knocking over a stack of old *National Geographics.* "I'm sure Robin would be happy to help you make an inventory."

Tracy considered this. Amy was right. Their cousin Robin Davisson owned an antique shop called Pearls of Wisdom, and she was their go-to when it came to questions about their attic finds. But she needn't think about that today. She wanted to find the footlocker containing Aunt Ruth's old jewelry box and keep an eye out for anything else that might be used in the pageant. Tracy recalled seeing strands of gold garland that could be used for halos for Jana and the other angels. She'd told Amy about it during lunch, and her sister had volunteered to venture into the attic to help search for it.

"Speaking of Robin," Amy went on, "I guess we won't be going over to her place to celebrate Kai's birthday this year. She said he doesn't want a party. How did he get to be fifteen so fast?" Amy shook her head.

"I don't know," Tracy said. "The kids all seem to grow up in such a hurry these days." She glanced at her watch. "Kai should be playing laser tag with his friends about now."

Kai had asked to skip his traditional birthday hot dog supper and family gathering for cake and ice cream. Instead, he'd requested a laser tag party with a couple of friends from school. This was the day that worked out for everyone, so Jeff and Robin's husband, Terry, had piled the boys into the SUV earlier that afternoon and headed to St. Louis.

"Jeff promised to spring for pizza after," Tracy added, "which was a great idea, because we didn't know what to get Kai for his birthday."

"I gave him a gift card. He can buy what he likes. I'm learning that the older they are, the harder it is to buy for them." Amy opened the drawers in a tall chest, peering inside each one. She pulled out a handful of worn and ratty doilies, yellowed with age, and put them back. "Robin said he's just as happy to have cash or a gift card and do his own shopping."

"Matt's probably getting to the age where he feels that way too," Tracy said. She picked up a small silver teapot, badly tarnished. After looking it over and noticing a dent, she put it down again. No wonder Robin hadn't claimed this for the store yet. Too much work involved to make it marketable.

"Matt's still hoping for that pinball machine he discovered at Robin's," Amy said. "I'd love to get it for him for Christmas, but it's too expensive. And with the thought of what the wedding will cost, I don't think I can afford it. Besides, what he really needs—and Jana too—is underwear, socks, and new pajamas."

"What a fun Santa's helper you are," Tracy teased. "Why don't you let me and Jeff give Matt and Jana those things for Christmas? You can give them the fun stuff. Oh, look." She pointed. "There it is."

Tracy shoved up the sleeves of her sweatshirt, made her way to the footlocker, and leaned over, heaving it away from the wall so Amy could open the lid. It made a rusty squeaking sound as she did so. The faint but pungent odor of mothballs wafted out of the trunk. Tracy wrinkled her nose. Such a nasty smell. She and Amy rummaged through the items stored inside. The wooden box with its domed lid was found easily enough. Amy removed it, along with an ivory-colored woolen bed jacket—worn and nubby with age. Tracy had a hard time imagining Aunt Ruth wearing it. Or had it been Grandma Pearl's?

"Hey, I can cut the sleeves off this and use it as part of a shepherd's costume," Amy said, sounding pleased.

"What about this?" Tracy lifted a brown waffle-weave blanket from the trunk. It was slightly moth-eaten, the satin binding frayed. "We could cut it up to make tunics for a couple of the kids."

Amy squealed. "Perfect. I'll take it."

Tracy glanced into the trunk and noticed an old scrapbook. The cardboard cover must have been navy blue at one time but had since faded to a sickly gray color. She lifted it and saw that the front and back covers were held together by thick black cords that looked like oversized shoelaces.

"What's this?" Tracy opened the book and started turning the heavy pages that were covered with old newspaper articles. The glue had dried out in places, leaving the articles loose and sometimes crumbling at the corners. There was a pink cameo brooch pinned to one of the stiff pages—the silver filigree tarnished with age. The profile of a young woman with cascading ringlets appeared to have been carved from ivory—real ivory or fake? Tracy didn't know which. The newspaper clippings had turned yellow. Some had puckered where the paste had dried underneath. The book smelled a bit musty. All the headlines and following articles shared a common theme: *Who Is the Woman in White?*

Each article—most of them from the *Lewis County Times* and a few from the *St. Louis Dispatch*—appeared to be about the death of an unidentified young woman. There was even a police sketch of her included with one article.

"Who is she?" Amy asked, peering over Tracy's shoulder.

"I don't know." Tracy read the caption, printed in bold capital letters. "'Police Seek Help in Identifying Deceased Woman.'"

"Are all the articles about the same thing?" Amy probed.

Tracy nodded. "I think so. I've only scanned the headlines, but they all seem to have something to do with this young woman who died in Canton, and no one knew who she was."

"When did this happen?"

Tracy noted a date in the corner of one of the articles. "December 1944."

"Then it can't be Aunt Ruth's scrapbook," Amy declared. "She wasn't even born yet."

Tracy frowned. "True. So maybe it was Grandma Pearl's."

Amy shrugged. "Or Grandpa Howard's."

Tracy chuckled. "I can't imagine Grandpa Howard sitting in the barracks somewhere with a jar of paste, cutting articles like this out of the newspaper."

With a smile, Amy admitted, "I guess you're right."

"Odd, though, that Grandma Pearl never mentioned this—if it belonged to her. Someone else could have cut out the articles and given the scrapbook to her." Tracy closed the book, determined to look at it more carefully later on. "Are you done rummaging through the trunk?"

Amy nodded.

Tracy hugged the scrapbook to her chest with one hand and closed the lid of the old trunk with the other.

"Grandma and Grandpa didn't talk much about World War II unless we prodded them," Amy pointed out. "And I don't remember Mom and Dad talking about the events of the fifties and sixties much." She shrugged as she gathered up the items she'd found. "Come to think of it, I'm not sure I've talked to Matt and Jana about 9/11 either—it gets mentioned at school, but we don't discuss it. If Grandma Pearl did keep that scrapbook, I suppose she could have eventually forgotten all about the incident surrounding the woman's death. It's not the kind of thing that comes up in daily conversation."

Tracy thought about that. Amy had a point.

They spent another fifteen minutes scrounging for odds and ends that might be useful for the pageant before making their way back downstairs. They found Aunt Ruth sitting on the couch in the living room, perusing Amy's three-ring binder—the one containing all the inspiration she'd gathered so far for her wedding.

"Hey, I thought you were going to sort through those Christmas decorations," Tracy said. She pointed to a box on the coffee table that she had brought down from the attic a week ago. With Christmas only two weeks away, it was time to finish decorating the old house the way Grandma Pearl used to. Aunt Ruth loved to help. Doing so brought back many fond memories for her. After all, she'd grown up in this house.

"I intended to." Aunt Ruth shrugged. "But I couldn't resist Amy's binder. You're so well organized," she said, smiling at her niece.

Amy smiled back. "I try. I really do."

Tracy held up the dusty scrapbook. "Ta-da! Look what we found in that old footlocker, Aunt Ruth."

"What is it, dear?"

Tracy thrust it toward her. "It's a scrapbook about some mysterious young woman who died in Canton back in December of 1944. Apparently, nobody knew who she was. Do you know if this belonged to Grandma Pearl? Did she cut out all the articles?"

Aunt Ruth took the scrapbook and opened it. As she touched the old cameo brooch, her eyes widened and she blinked rapidly. Her mouth dropped open, her shoulders began to shake, and to Tracy's dismay, her aunt burst into tears.

A Note from the Editors

We hope you enjoyed another exciting volume in the Secrets from Grandma's Attic series, published by Guideposts. For over seventy-five years Guideposts, a nonprofit organization, has been driven by a vision of a world filled with hope. We aspire to be the voice of a trusted friend, a friend who makes you feel more hopeful and connected.

By making a purchase from Guideposts, you join our community in touching millions of lives, inspiring them to believe that all things are possible through faith, hope, and prayer. Your continued support allows us to provide uplifting resources to those in need. Whether through our online communities, websites, apps, or publications, we strive to inspire our audiences, bring them together, comfort, uplift, entertain, and guide them.

To learn more, please go to guideposts.org.

Find inspiration, find faith, find Guideposts.

Shop our bestsellers and favorites at
guideposts.org/shop

Or scan the QR code to go directly to our Shop

While you are waiting for the next fascinating story in Secrets from Grandma's Attic, check out some other Guideposts mystery series!

Savannah Secrets

Welcome to Savannah, Georgia, a picture-perfect Southern city known for its manicured parks, moss-covered oaks, and antebellum architecture. Walk down one of the cobblestone streets, and you'll come upon Magnolia Investigations. It is here where two friends have joined forces to unravel some of Savannah's deepest secrets. Tag along as clues are exposed, red herrings discarded, and thrilling surprises revealed. Find inspiration in the special bond between Meredith Bellefontaine and Julia Foley. Cheer the friends on as they listen to their hearts and rely on their faith to solve each new case that comes their way.

The Hidden Gate
A Fallen Petal
Double Trouble
Whispering Bells
Where Time Stood Still
The Weight of Years
Willful Transgressions

Season's Meetings
Southern Fried Secrets
The Greatest of These
Patterns of Deception
The Waving Girl
Beneath a Dragon Moon
Garden Variety Crimes
Meant for Good
A Bone to Pick
Honeybees & Legacies
True Grits
Sapphire Secret
Jingle Bell Heist
Buried Secrets
A Puzzle of Pearls
Facing the Facts
Resurrecting Trouble
Forever and a Day

Mysteries of Martha's Vineyard

Priscilla Latham Grant has inherited a lighthouse! So with not much more than a strong will and a sore heart, the recent widow says goodbye to her lifelong Kansas home and heads to the quaint and historic island of Martha's Vineyard, Massachusetts. There, she comes face-to-face with adventures, which include her trusty canine friend, Jake, three delightful cousins she didn't know she had, and Gerald O'Bannon, a handsome Coast Guard captain—plus head-scratching mysteries that crop up with surprising regularity.

A Light in the Darkness
Like a Fish Out of Water
Adrift
Maiden of the Mist
Making Waves
Don't Rock the Boat
A Port in the Storm
Thicker Than Water
Swept Away
Bridge Over Troubled Waters
Smoke on the Water
Shifting Sands

Shark Bait
Seascape in Shadows
Storm Tide
Water Flows Uphill
Catch of the Day
Beyond the Sea
Wider Than an Ocean
Sheeps Passing in the Night
Sail Away Home
Waves of Doubt
Lifeline
Flotsam & Jetsam
Just Over the Horizon

Find more inspiring stories in these best-loved Guideposts fiction series!

Mysteries of Lancaster County
Follow the Classen sisters as they unravel clues and uncover hidden secrets in Mysteries of Lancaster County. As you get to know these women and their friends, you'll see how God brings each of them together for a fresh start in life.

Secrets of Wayfarers Inn
Retired schoolteachers find themselves owners of an old warehouse-turned-inn that is filled with hidden passages, buried secrets, and stunning surprises that will set them on a course to puzzling mysteries from the Underground Railroad.

Tearoom Mysteries Series
Mix one stately Victorian home, a charming lakeside town in Maine, and two adventurous cousins with a passion for tea and hospitality. Add a large scoop of intriguing mystery, and sprinkle generously with faith, family, and friends, and you have the recipe for *Tearoom Mysteries*.

Ordinary Women of the Bible
Richly imagined stories—based on facts from the Bible—have all the plot twists and suspense of a great mystery, while bringing you fascinating insights on what it was like to be a woman living in the ancient world.

To learn more about these books, visit Guideposts.org/Shop